Mastering
The Macintosh™
Toolbox

David B. Peatroy
and
DATATECH Publications

Osborne McGraw-Hill
Berkeley, California

Published by
Osborne **McGraw-Hill**
2600 Tenth Street
Berkeley, California 94710
U.S.A.

For information on translations and book distributors outside of the U.S.A., please write to Osborne **McGraw-Hill** at the above address.

Macintosh, MacWrite, and MacPaint are trademarks of Apple Computer, Inc.
Apple is a registered trademark of Apple Computer, Inc.
IBM is a registered trademark of International Business Machines Corp.

Mastering
the Macintosh™ Toolbox

1234567890   DODO   8998765

ISBN 0-07-881203-8

Jonathan Erickson, Acquisitions Editor   Deborah Wilson, Composition
Paul Jensen, Technical Editor   Yashi Okita, Cover Design
Carol Hamilton, Copy Editor   Jan Benes, Text Design

C O N T E N T S

A C K N O W L E D G M E N T S

The author would like to acknowledge the following people and companies for their support and assistance in the preparation of this book:

Mike Burns, Think Technologies, for providing technical information about programming in Macintosh Pascal.

Bryan J. Cummings, DATATECH Publications, for providing technical assistance, hours of manuscript preparation, preliminary document preparation, and final organization.

Barbara Koalkin, Apple Computer, Inc., for supplying the Macintosh Pascal software disk, documentation, and assistance.

Arnold Kunert, DATATECH Publications, for coordinating the editing, restructuring, and organization of the text.

Alexis Peatroy, my loving wife, for those times I needed her most.

Lawrence Pollack, DATATECH Publications, for providing numerous hours of instruction in the finer points of Pascal.

For Mum and Alexis

INTRODUCTION

On January 22nd, 1984, during the broadcast of the eighteenth Superbowl, a television commercial with a strangely Orwellian quality was seen by millions of people across the United States. The commercial was subsequently discussed in network newscasts and reported upon in major newspapers and magazines. The news? Apple Computer, Inc., of Cupertino, California, had just unveiled its Macintosh computer.

The Macintosh is not just another personal computer in an already overcrowded marketplace. The philosophy behind the Macintosh is to bring the power of a personal computer to the vast majority of people who have neither the time nor the inclination to learn what it takes to operate a conventional computer effectively.

The Macintosh, unlike other popular computers, is intended to be the first "intuitive" personal computer. Its operation is designed to be as simple as possible, with the required instructions needed to run the machine always close at hand. In this respect, the Macintosh is vastly different from other personal computers.

The Macintosh and its software are designed to *inform* the person using it. And as such, Macintosh software neither resembles nor behaves like software written for a machine like, for example, the IBM PC. Whereas the IBM requires the person using the computer to type commands through a keyboard into the computer to perform a task, the Macintosh uses pictures, called icons, that represent commonly used functions and items, and pull-down menus, that list all the commands available at a given time. The chief benefit of Apple's approach is that a complete novice can, with a little perseverance and common sense, put a machine like the Macintosh to use much more quickly than he or she could an IBM PC.

Of course, the way the Macintosh interacts with its user and performs its tasks is through a combination of software and hardware. Software allows us to communicate with the computer, letting us tell it what we want to do, then carrying out our instructions. Hardware lets us communicate our instructions to the software within the computer. Perhaps the most unusual feature of the Macintosh's hardware, next to its dazzling on-screen graphics, is the mouse, a rolling desktop pointer that allows users to bypass the need to type commands at the keyboard and lets them carry out operations simply by selecting commands with the pointer on the screen.

It is beyond the scope of this book to teach you all you need to know about Macintosh software and how to write it. However, this book will show you that learning to write software is not difficult and that learning to program the Macintosh can be an extremely enjoyable pastime.

This book concentrates on the interaction of the mouse with the computer and demonstrates how best to utilize the mouse for functions like menu control and graphics. The programming language chosen for this book is Macintosh Pascal. *Mastering the Macintosh Toolbox* assumes that you have at least a rudimentary understanding of Pascal and are familiar with some version of the language on either a personal computer or minicomputer.

Pascal has been chosen for two reasons. First, it is one of a few languages available for the Macintosh that is sophisticated enough to take full advantage of the Toolbox, the Macintosh's internal wellspring of programming routines, aids, and other intrinsic hardware capabilities. Second, Pascal is a terrific language to learn because it encourages the principles of sound and logical programming.

This book assumes that you are familiar with the Macintosh environment of windows, pull-down menus, selections, and the mouse. If you are unsure of how the Macintosh environment works, you should familiarize yourself with it by using applications programs like MacWrite and MacPaint. Aside from being easy and fun to use, these programs beautifully illustrate the concepts behind the Macintosh.

You will also find a reference section comprised of three appendixes to satisfy your demand for quick answers to syntax and usage questions about Macintosh Pascal. Of course, the final authority is the reference guide that comes with Macintosh Pascal.

1

Getting Started

There are many reasons for learning to program a computer. Some people learn to program because they are considering a career in computers. Others learn to program because they require a specific piece of software for which there is no commercially available counterpart. Some want to learn to program so they can customize software that is available for another computer, but not their own. In short, there are probably as many reasons to learn to program a computer as there are computer users. Learning to program a computer is not that difficult; like eating an elephant, it must be done one *byte* at a time.

Just as there are many reasons for learning to program a computer, there are many things that a computer may be programmed to do. Bookkeeping and accounting are two popular examples. Word processing, using a computer to write and edit text, is a requirement for many. Some people like to use their computers for entertainment, and some even write their own games. Parents often use computers to teach their children educational basics and to familiarize them with computer use.

The Macintosh is particularly suited to various kinds of programs because of its inherent ease of use and the relative ease with which a programmer can create remarkable graphics.

Many of the programs that create the unique look of the Macintosh are available to the programmer working with Macintosh Pascal. These programs are located in what is called the *Toolbox;* they make up part of what is known as the *Macintosh User Interface*. A user interface is the way the person using the computer, the user, communicates with the computer. The Toolbox programs help control the look of the Macintosh windows, allow the use of the desk accessories, control the mouse, and govern the overall appearance of the Macintosh desktop. In fact, there are about 500 different Toolbox programs stored in a special area of the Macintosh's Read-Only memory (ROM).

Commercial Macintosh programs (also called applications) like MacWrite and MacPaint are generally developed on an Apple Lisa computer using a special Pascal development language. Once written, the programs are transported to the Macintosh. The Macintosh Pascal used throughout this book is not a complete development Pascal. It has direct access to some, but not all, of the support programs contained in the Toolbox. As a result, programs written on the Macintosh with Macintosh Pascal run more slowly than commercially developed programs and contain limited use of such special Macintosh features as windows and menus.

Interpreters versus Compilers

Macintosh programs written with the Lisa Pascal development system use a *compiled* version of Pascal. Compiled programs take the *source code* written by a programmer and convert it into what is called *native code*. Native code is the most fundamental language with which we can communicate with a computer; it consists entirely of 1's and 0's. While native code produces the fastest executable code on a computer, it is too tedious to program entire applications with. Therefore, languages like Pascal, called *high-level* languages, were developed to allow programs to be written in an English-like language and then converted, by the compiler, into the native code of the computer. Lisa Pascal, like all previous versions of Pascal, is compiled.

While compiled versions of programs are preferred for commercial applications like spreadsheets and word processors, compiling programs can be a tedious technical process, especially for someone just learning to program. Therefore, *interpreters* were developed to make creating and running programs a simple two-step process. The programmer types in his or her program (the source code) and then uses a command to run the program. The steps of compiling are eliminated. The result is a program that can be run instantly. The penalty paid for using the interpreter is that interpreted programs run more slowly than their compiled counterparts. In some cases, they run significantly slower. Thus, interpreted languages are great teaching aids but are not suited for commercial program development where speed of execution is crucial.

The most popular interpreted computer language is BASIC. Nearly every personal computer has a variety of BASIC that runs on it. Like these versions of BASIC, Macintosh Pascal is interpreted. It breaks with the tradition of Pascal being a compiled language and introduces an interpreted version that is ideally suited for learning to program in Pascal in general and on the Macintosh in particular. Programs written with Macintosh Pascal may be converted to Lisa Pascal programs with a minimum of effort. This makes Macintosh Pascal useful for determining the feasibility of a particular program on the Macintosh before investment in a complete development system.

One small drawback of using Macintosh Pascal is its lack of access to some of the routines contained in the Toolbox. This is because the interpreter running Macintosh Pascal is itself an applications program running under control of the various routines contained in the Toolbox. Therefore, programs written with Macintosh Pascal could make use of Toolbox routines that affect the Pascal interpreter. The result could be erratic program execution or even a complete shutdown or *crash* of the computer. But don't let this knowledge make you timid when you program. The developers of Macintosh Pascal have taken every precaution to prevent you from inadvertently using Toolbox routines that would adversely affect the Pascal interpreter.

Inside the Macintosh User Interface

The programs in the Macintosh User Interface are split up into several discrete packages called *Managers*. Figure 1-1 shows the relative relationships between these programs.

Reading up from the bottom of Figure 1-1, here is a brief description of what each program does.

The *Resource Manager* coordinates the use of resources. Resources are data that may be used by a program when it is running. This data is kept separate from the program code. Examples of resources are font definitions, menus, icons, and text strings. The Resource Manager routines are usually called by the routines from such higher packages as the Font Manager and the Menu Manager.

The *Font Manager* supports the use of multiple text fonts. It calls the Resource Manager when it needs a font not already in memory. Routines in the Font Manager are used to control the size and style of the font in use. The Font Manager routines are usually called from QuickDraw routines.

QuickDraw is the graphics package that is at the heart of both the Macintosh and the Lisa. The most obvious example of QuickDraw's capacity is found in MacPaint. Both QuickDraw and MacPaint were written by Apple's Bill Atkinson.

The *Event Manager* is a program's connection to the outside world. The movements of the mouse, keys pressed on the keyboard, and the use of the mouse button are all reported to a program via the Event Manager.

The *Toolbox Utilities* are programs that handle miscellaneous tasks like working with text (string operations) and fixed point arithmetic.

The *Window Manager* controls the appearance of windows. Since the Macintosh's displays occur in windows, this is a very important package. The Window Manager takes care of the housekeeping, thus allowing a program to interact with windows at a very high level. Housekeeping functions include drawing window borders, moving windows around and resizing them, and redrawing the various areas of windows that need to be redrawn when, for example, windows that overlap are moved around the screen. There are different types of windows that can be used by the programmer, some of which may be used by the applications being written and others that may be used by higher packages like the Menu Manager or the Dialog Manager.

The *Control Manager* governs the use of software buttons, check boxes, and dials. These items allow the user to make and confirm decisions regarding essential operations like printing, saving files, and exiting applications. Within an applications program, buttons, boxes, and dials change the value of variables that control the way a program reacts. For instance, a check box may be used to determine whether the program prints to the screen or to the printer.

The *Menu Manager* uses a two-dimensional array to control the appearance of the menus that you normally see at the top of the Macintosh screen. The Apple, File, Edit, View, and Special menus listed at the top of the screen on the Macintosh desktop are an example of menus governed by the Menu Manager. The Menu Manager allows a program to create a set of menus and display it on the screen. Once a menu is activated with the mouse, the Menu Manager

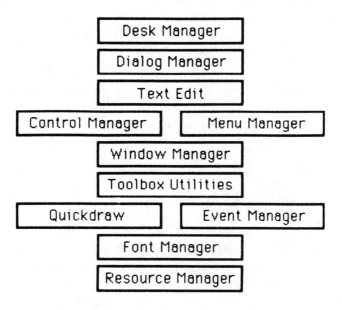

Figure 1-1. *Relative relationships of Macintosh User Interface Managers*

takes control from the applications program until a selection is made. Once a selection is made, the Menu Manager reports the selection to the program.

The *Text Edit* package performs elementary text entry and editing. Text Edit is designed so that an applications program may modify its behavior. A package that is not contained in ROM but is on the disk is the Core Edit, which is more sophisticated. Core Edit, which must be loaded into memory first, can handle different fonts, styles, and sizes.

The *Dialog Manager* controls dialog boxes that appear when the Macintosh requires more information in order to continue a task. A common dialog box is the one displayed when you select Open from the File menu in MacWrite. Another common dialog box is the one displayed when Save or Save As is selected from the File menu of MacPaint. Dialog boxes prompt the user to enter the information required by the program to continue.

The *Desk Manager* is used by an applications program to access the desk accessories that usually sit under the Apple menu as part of the program itself. Desk accessories are actually little programs that are stored as resources on disk. If a user selects a desk accessory, the applications program passes control to the Desk Manager, which takes care of loading and starting the selected desk accessory. Desk accessories may take many forms, such as the calculator, alarm clock, and the note pad listed in the Apple menu on several versions of the Finder.

Pascal Basics

Before actually writing our first Macintosh Pascal program, let's briefly review and define some standard Pascal terminology. Pascal is a *block-oriented language*. This means that you divide your programming into small, single-purpose units. Each unit or block is (ideally) designed so that it performs a single or small group of related tasks, such as adding a series of numbers and computing their average, or drawing a graphics image on the screen.

The Pascal constructs that allow the writing of program blocks are the *procedure* and the *function*. Essentially, procedures and functions are programs within the main Pascal program that may themselves contain other procedures and functions. Procedures pass information like variables and constants back and forth between the parts of the program calling the procedure. Functions behave in a similar fashion except that they may be used to compute and return a single result to the calling part of the program.

The routines in the Toolbox are called from Pascal in the form of procedures and functions. Unlike procedures and functions that you create in a Pascal program, the Toolbox routines are *predefined* within the ROM of the Macintosh and may be used anywhere in a program without being first declared. Pascal provides you with access to these predefined functions and procedures as if you had written them yourself. In this sense, they behave like other built-in Pascal procedures, such as Write and Read.

Along with the predefined functions and procedures of the Toolbox come predefined data types. Like the Toolbox procedures and functions, these data types may be used directly within Macintosh Pascal programs and need not be declared.

Starting Macintosh Pascal

Turn on your Macintosh and insert the Macintosh Pascal disk in the internal disk drive. When the desktop appears, open the disk window by selecting Open from the File menu. Then select the Macintosh Pascal icon by clicking on it with the mouse pointer. Choose Open again from the File menu to start Macintosh Pascal. Figure 1-2 shows what you will see when Pascal is ready to use. Use the mouse to position the insertion point in front of the word "begin" in the Untitled window. Then type

```
var
Window:Rect;
```

Press the RETURN key to end a line and start a new one. Now place the insertion point in front of the word "end" and type

```
HideAll;
SetRect (Window, 0, 38, 511, 341);
SetDrawingRect (Window);
ShowDrawing;
```

Note that entering and editing programs in Macintosh Pascal is

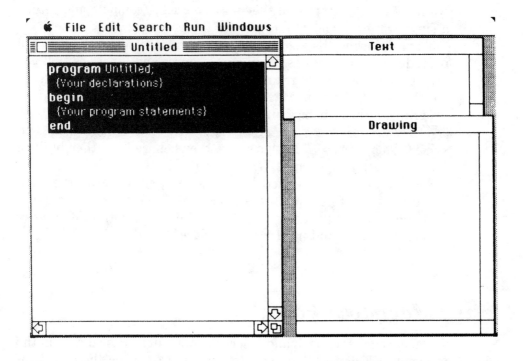

Figure 1-2. *Screen display when Pascal is ready to use*

similar to writing with MacWrite. The same rules apply regarding placement of the insertion point, text selection, and cutting or copying of text to the Clipboard. If you are unfamiliar with the basics of text editing on the Macintosh, you should refer to the chapter entitled "Using Macintosh Pascal" in the *Macintosh Pascal User's Guide.*

To run this Macintosh Pascal program, simply go to the Run menu and select the Go option. Your program should reproduce the screen shown in Figure 1-3, providing you typed everything into the computer correctly.

If you made a typing error, a box with a ladybug appears on your screen. Click inside the box to proceed, check your spelling and punctuation, and try to run the program again. Macintosh Pascal requires strict use of correct spelling of keywords and the proper usage of all punctuation (upper- or lowercase characters do not have

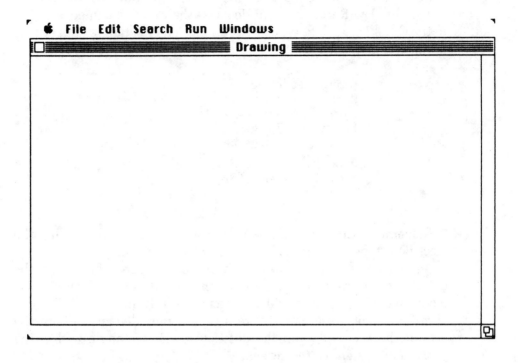

Figure 1-3.   *Screen display after selection of Go option*

any significance). If you did have a problem when you tried to run this program, a pointing finger will lead you to the location of the problem in your program. This is one of the nicest features of Macintosh Pascal. It points out your errors so that you can set about correcting them immediately.

What does this program do? If you shrink the Drawing window using the size box at the lower right corner of the window and drag it back to its original position, you will see that the Untitled window and the Text window have disappeared. Don't panic. They can be reopened from the Windows menu. Their disappearance was the result of the first procedure call in the program, HideAll. In executing this statement, Macintosh Pascal calls a predefined procedure within the Toolbox that closes all open windows.

The Drawing window is the result of the rest of the first program. It tells the Macintosh to set the size of a window and to display that window on the screen using the predefined SetRect procedure.

Let's examine in detail each line of the program that you typed.

The Window:Rect statement declares the variable named Window to the QuickDraw data type of Rectangle. The Rectangle data type is defined as follows:

```
type Rect =  record case integer of
        0: (top:         integer;
            left:        integer;
            bottom:      integer;
            right:       integer);

        1: (topLeft:     Point;
            botRight:    Point)
    end;
```

Remember, this declaration is for your reference when using the Rect data type. It need not be declared by you in a program.

As can be seen above, Rect may be four integers specifying the coordinates of two points that define the two corners of the rectangle (coordinates and points will be discussed fully in Chapter 2). The significance of these four integers is that they determine both the size of the rectangle and the position of the rectangle within the coordinate system of the screen.

The SetRect statement is used to set the window boundaries. There are 512 pixels (black or white picture elements or dots) across the Macintosh screen (columns) and 342 pixels down (rows).

SetRect is defined as

```
Procedure SetRect (var r:Rect; left, top, right, bottom:integer);
```

In the program the statement SetRect (Window,0,38,511,341) stores the numbers for left, top, right, and bottom into the record variable Window. The result is a window with the coordinates on the screen specified by the four integers.

The specific numbers used in this program set the boundaries of the window just below the menu bar and use the rest of the screen for the rectangle. After the size of the window has been determined, the Macintosh must be told that this is to be the size of the Drawing window.

The SetDrawingRect (Window) statement sets the Drawing window equal to the bounds specified by the variable Window. The last statement, ShowDrawing, simply tells the Macintosh to display the

Drawing window, which covers almost the entire screen but leaves the menu bar visible.

The Drawing window in Macintosh Pascal may be any size specified by the SetRect statement. It may even be larger than the Macintosh screen. Play around with the program, altering the size of the window by changing the numbers in the SetRect statement. By using SetRect (Window,100,200,200,300), the Macintosh will open a Drawing window in the center of the screen.

A program similar to the first can be used to control the Text window of Macintosh Pascal. The procedures required to do this are SetTextRect and ShowText. They operate in exactly the same way as the SetDrawingRect and ShowDrawing procedures. The program statements below work in a manner similar to the first program.

```
HideAll;
SetRect (Window, 0, 38, 511, 341);
SetTextRect (Window);
ShowText;
```

Type these lines into the main program body of the Untitled window or make the necessary modifications to your old program. Make sure to leave the original variable declaration from the first program intact. Run the program and you will see a screen similar to the one created by the first program, but this time the Text window, not the Drawing window, is on the screen.

In Macintosh Pascal the Text window is used as the standard text output file. Text-oriented procedures such as Write and Writeln send their output to the Text window. The Drawing window is a Quick-Draw grafPort (grafPorts will be defined later). It is the window that QuickDraw uses for its output. The Drawing window can display any graphics or text that is originated by QuickDraw procedures.

The DrawBoxes Program

After having experimented with this first program, you may want to save your modified program for later use. If so, select Save As in the File menu. Macintosh Pascal will prompt you to name the program. Once named, you can close the program window and select "New" from the File menu to open an Untitled program window. Clear any text in the Untitled window by selecting it and pressing the BACK-

SPACE key. Then type in the following program exactly as it appears:

```
program DrawBoxes;
  var
    Window : Rect;
    But1, But2, But3, But4 : Rect;
  procedure InitWindow;
  begin
    HideAll;
    SetRect(Window, 0, 38, 511, 341);
    SetDrawingRect(Window);
    ShowDrawing;
  end;
  procedure SetButtons;
  begin
    SetRect(But1, 25, 70, 40, 80);
    SetRect(But2, 25, 90, 40, 100);
    SetRect(But3, 25, 110, 40, 120);
    SetRect(But4, 25, 130, 40, 140);
  end;
  procedure SetPen;
  begin
    PenNormal;
  end;
  procedure DrawButtons;
  begin
    FrameRect(but1);
    FrameRect(but2);
    FrameRect(but3);
    FrameRect(but4);
  end;
begin
  SetButtons;
  InitWindow;
  SetPen;
  DrawButtons;
end.
```

After you have typed in the above program, verify that spelling and punctuation are correct. Use the Check option in the Run menu to have Macintosh Pascal read your program without trying to run it. Any mistakes will be pointed out and you can fix them before running the program.

Once you know the program is correct, select Go from the Run menu to run the program. Figure 1-4 shows a screen display generated by the DrawBoxes program.

This screen display looks primitive compared to what you're

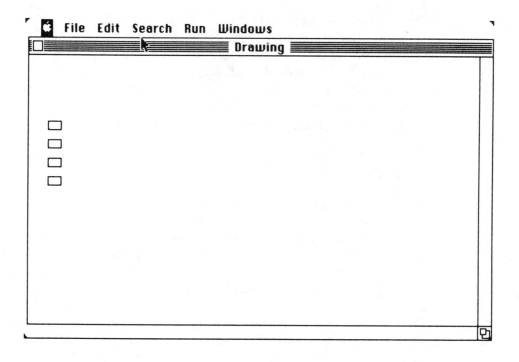

Figure 1-4. *Screen display generated by DrawBoxes program*

accustomed to seeing on the Macintosh, but let's examine how it was created.

The procedure InitWindow sets the size of the Drawing window and displays it.

Notice the new variables, But1, But2, But3, and But4 of type Rect. These are initialized using the SetRect statement in the procedure SetButtons.

Now look at the procedure SetPen. It has one statement in it— PenNormal. PenNormal sets the QuickDraw graphics pen to its normal or default settings. PenNormal does not affect the location of the graphics pen, however.

QuickDraw uses a conceptual pen to draw images on the Macintosh screen. The pen has a number of features that may be altered by the programmer. You may visualize the pen as represented in Figure 1-5.

The pen has the attributes of position, height, width, and pattern. In addition, the pen may be either visible or invisible—that is, it may draw on the screen or it may not (writing in "invisible ink"). For now, note the features of position, height, width, and pattern. We will be using them and showing how they are affected by the Pen-Normal statement in the program.

PenNormal sets the following graphics pen attributes:

```
Pen height  = 1 bit
Pen width   = 1 bit
Pen pattern = black
Pen mode    = PatCopy
```

The mode PatCopy simply means that the pen will replace whatever is already on the screen with the pen pattern. In this case, the pattern is black. The pen pattern serves as the ink in the pen. In the example above, the pen will draw a thin black line 1 bit wide and 1 bit high.

The next step in the DrawBoxes program is to tell the pen what to draw and where to draw it. Looking at the procedure DrawButtons,

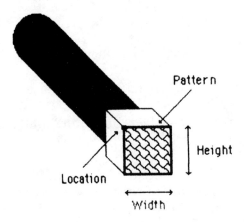

Figure 1-5.   Conceptual pen used by QuickDraw

you see a call to the procedure FrameRect. This statement tells QuickDraw to draw the outline of a rectangle. The variables But1, But2, But3, and But4 of type Rect tell the procedure where to place the rectangle and its size.

As with the first program, try altering the sizes and positions of the boxes by changing the numbers in the SetButtons procedure.

The DrawButtons Program

What follows is another program that utilizes some of the basic concepts discussed so far, but takes them one small step further. Save the DrawBoxes program so that you may refer to it later. Then type the following into Macintosh Pascal:

```
program DrawButtons;
  var
    Window : Rect;
    Button : Rect;
  procedure InitWindow;
  begin
    SetRect(Window, 0, 38, 511, 341);
    SetDrawingRect(Window);
    ShowDrawing;
  end;
  procedure SetButton;
  begin
    SetRect(Button, 240, 40, 270, 60);
  end;
  procedure SetPen;
  begin
    PenNormal;
    PenSize(2, 2);
  end;
  procedure DrawButtons;
    var
      I : Integer;
  begin
    for I := 1 to 4 do
      begin
        OffsetRect(Button, 0, 30);
        FrameRect(Button);
      end;
  end;
  procedure LabelButtons;
  begin
    TextFont(0);
```

```
    TextMode(srcOr);
    TextSize(0);
    MoveTo(252, 85);
    DrawChar('A');
    MoveTo(252, 115);
    DrawChar('B');
    MoveTo(252, 145);
    DrawChar('C');
    MoveTo(252, 175);
    DrawChar('D');
  end;
begin
  SetButton;
  InitWindow;
  SetPen;
  DrawButtons;
  LabelButtons;
end.
```

using and moving pen

After typing in the program, select the Go option from the Run menu to execute the DrawButtons program. The program produces the screen shown in Figure 1-6.

The most important difference between this program and the DrawBoxes program is the use of the OffsetRect procedure. Quick-Draw provides a number of procedures that perform calculations on rectangles, and OffsetRect is one of the most useful. The OffsetRect procedure lets you change the position of a rectangle without affecting its size. The procedure OffsetRect is defined as follows:

procedure OffsetRect (var r:Rect; dh, dv:integer);

where r is any variable of type Rect, dh is the horizontal distance to move the rectangle, and dv is the vertical distance to move the rectangle.

OffsetRect uses positive values for dh to indicate movement to the right and dv to indicate movement downward. Negative values indicate movement to the left and upward.

In examining the SetPen procedure, you will notice the PenSize statement. PenSize is a predefined procedure that is used to set the size of the graphics pen. The definition of PenSize is

procedure PenSize (width, height:integer);

Both the width and the height may range from (0,0) to (32767,32767). It should be noted that if either the width or the

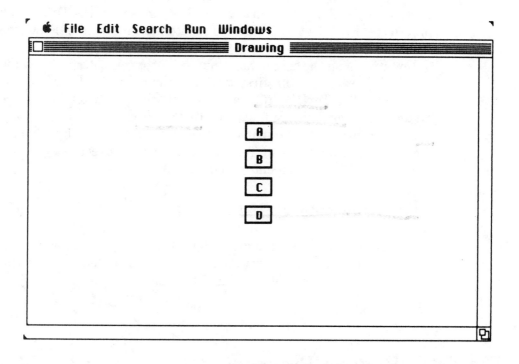

Figure 1-6.   *Screen display produced by DrawButtons program*

height is less than 1, the pen will not draw on the screen. After the pen size has been set, the pen will use the new dimensions. In DrawButtons, the new pen size affects the FrameRect procedure, which produces the outline of the buttons.

The last major item to notice in the DrawButtons program is the procedure LabelButtons. This illustrates the use of single text characters to label the buttons we have already drawn. The graphics pen is also responsible for drawing text on the screen, although the mode of use is a little different. MoveTo is a procedure that, when called, will move the graphics pen to the specified location. It is defined as

procedure MoveTo (h, v:integer);

where *h* is the horizontal coordinate and *v* is the vertical coordinate. MoveTo does not draw on the screen.

In DrawButtons, the position of the pen after the first MoveTo statement will be slightly to the left of the center of the top button. This is where the first character will be drawn by the DrawChar procedure. Each successive MoveTo statement moves the pen to the next button to be labeled.

Text drawn on the screen has a number of special attributes, some of which are set by the first two statements of the LabelButtons procedure. The TextFont(0) statement sets the character font to the system font (the Chicago font) and TextSize(0) sets the point size to 12. The DrawChar statement will draw text in the 12 point Chicago font after TextFont(0) and TextSize(0) have been executed.

The DrawChar statement is defined as

```
procedure DrawChar (ch:char);
```

This statement draws the character specified by *ch* at the current location of the pen. Once DrawChar has been executed, the pen will be located to the right of the character just drawn.

The ActiveButtons Program

As can be seen from the screen produced by running DrawButtons, there are four centrally located buttons labeled A, B, C, and D. Now that you've walked through the steps required to create buttons, the next logical step is to demonstrate the effect of using the mouse within a program. Type Active Buttons into Macintosh Pascal after having saved the previous program for your reference and later use.

```
program ActiveButtons;
  var
    R : Rect;
    But1, But2, But3, But4 : Rect;
    MousePos : Point;
  procedure InitWindow;
  begin
    SetRect(R, 0, 38, 511, 341);
    SetDrawingRect(R);
    ShowDrawing;
  end;
  procedure SetButtons;
```

```
begin
  SetRect(But1, 240, 70, 270, 90);
  SetRect(But2, 240, 100, 270, 120);
  SetRect(But3, 240, 130, 270, 150);
  SetRect(But4, 240, 160, 270, 180);
end;
procedure SetPen;
begin
  PenNormal;
  PenSize(2, 2);
end;
procedure DrawButtons;
begin
  FrameRect(but1);
  FrameRect(but2);
  FrameRect(but3);
  FrameRect(but4);
end;
procedure LabelButtons;
begin
  TextFont(0);
  TextMode(srcOr);
  TextSize(0);
  MoveTo(252, 85);
  DrawChar('A');
  MoveTo(252, 115);
  DrawChar('B');
  MoveTo(252, 145);
  DrawChar('C');
  MoveTo(252, 175);
  DrawChar('D');
end;
begin
  SetButtons;
  InitWindow;
  SetPen;
  DrawButtons;
  LabelButtons;
  repeat
  until Button;
  GetMouse(MousePos.h, MousePos.v);
  if PtInRect(MousePos, But1) then
    begin
      InvertRect(But1);
      SysBeep(10);
      InvertRect(But1);
      MoveTo(180, 220);
      Textfont(1);
      DrawString('Button A has been pressed');
    end;
  if PtInRect(MousePos, But2) then
    begin
      InvertRect(But2);
```

```
          SysBeep(10);
          InvertRect(But2);
          MoveTo(180, 220);
          Textfont(1);
          DrawString('Button B has been pressed');
       end;
    if PtInRect(MousePos, But3) then
       begin
          InvertRect(But3);
          SysBeep(10);
          InvertRect(But3);
          MoveTo(180, 220);
          Textfont(1);
          DrawString('Button C has been pressed');
       end;
    if PtInRect(MousePos, But4) then
       begin
          InvertRect(But4);
          SysBeep(10);
          InvertRect(But4);
          MoveTo(180, 220);
          Textfont(1);
          DrawString('Button D has been pressed');
       end;
    end.
```

When run, this program displays the screen shown in Figure 1-7 and waits until the mouse button is pressed. If the cursor is located within one of the four buttons when the mouse button is pressed, the button will flash, the Macintosh will beep, and you will be informed at the bottom of the screen which button was selected by the mouse. If the cursor is not located inside a button when the mouse button is pressed, nothing will happen. The program ends after the mouse button has been pressed once.

After the LabelButtons procedure has been executed, the initialization of the screen is complete and the program will continuously loop until Button becomes True. Button is a Boolean function that will return True if the mouse button is currently down and False if it isn't. The program effectively waits until the mouse button is pressed. Once the mouse button has been pressed, the first statement to be executed is the GetMouse statement. This procedure returns the position of the mouse. It is defined as

procedure GetMouse (h,v:integer);

where h contains the returned horizontal coordinate and v contains the returned vertical coordinate. Our program uses the .h and .v

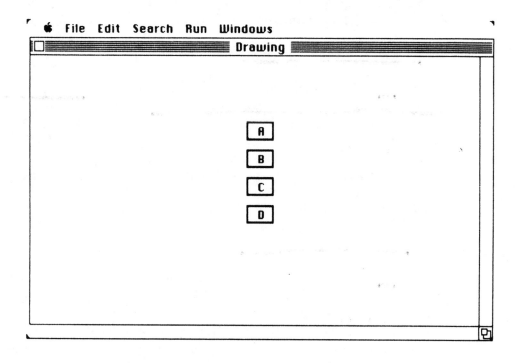

Figure 1-7. *Screen display produced by ActiveButtons program*

definition of a point, so that the point MousePos represents the position of the mouse when the mouse button was pressed. (See the definition of the Point data type in the *Macintosh Pascal Reference Manual*.) The remainder of the program consists of four If statements. Each If statement tests the position of the mouse to determine whether or not the mouse pointer is within a button on the screen when the button is pressed. The function that makes this test is PtInRect. It is defined as

function PtInRect (pt:Point; r:Rect):boolean;

PtInRect is a Boolean function that returns True if the point specified by *pt* is located within the rectangle specified by *r*. This procedure is used within ActiveButtons to test whether or not the mouse is within one of the screen buttons when the mouse button is pressed. The statements within the block following each If statement determine the action of the program after the button has been identified.

Procedure SysBeep is a Pascal procedure that "rings" the Macintosh speaker. It is defined as

procedure SysBeep (d:integer);

where _d_ is the duration of the sound. The duration is measured in increments of approximately 0.022 seconds. Therefore, if d is set equal to 10, then the sound will continue for approximately 2/10ths of a second.

The flash of each button is caused by using the InvertRect procedure, which will invert each pixel within a given rectangle. Inversion simply converts every white pixel into a black pixel and every black pixel into a white one. The procedure is defined as

procedure InvertRect (r:Rect);

where _r_ is the rectangle that will be inverted. In ActiveButtons, because you want the button to flash, there are two InvertRect statements (to repeat the inversion twice). Notice that InvertRect retains the contents of the rectangle so that any label character is unaffected, even though it flashes with the rest of the rectangle. InvertRect does not affect the graphics pen in any way.

The last section of the If statement branch tells us which button on the screen was pressed by writing the information on the screen. It uses a procedure similar to the one used to label the buttons. The DrawString procedure, defined as

procedure DrawString (s:Str255);

draws the string specified by _s_ at the current location of the graphics pen. After the procedure has been executed, the pen is positioned to the right of the string drawn. As with the DrawChar procedure used to label the buttons, you must use the MoveTo procedure to position the pen prior to the next call of the DrawString procedure.

Notice the TextFont(1) statement that is executed prior to the DrawString procedure. This procedure changes the font the string is drawn in. The Macintosh allows text to be displayed on the screen in any number of different fonts stored in the System file. TextFont allows us to control which font is currently in use. The font number is used by the Toolbox routines to determine which font should be used. The following table equates font numbers to the font names with which you are probably more familiar:

Font Number	Font Name
0	Chicago (System Font)
1	ApplFont (Application Font)
2	New York
3	Geneva
4	Monaco
5	Venice
6	London
7	Athens
8	San Francisco
9	Toronto

Font numbers 0 and 1 have special implications in that they are used slightly differently by Macintosh. Font number 1 is not actually a font, but rather a pointer, or reference, to another font used by applications. This pointer varies with different releases of the Macintosh Finder, but it will point to either the New York or Geneva fonts. Font number 0 is used as the system font, which is the font used for the menu bar and menu commands. This font also has some special characters that are used by the system, such as the apple used to identify the Apple menu.

The ActiveButtons program is a basic example of the use of the mouse to control a program that has many options. With slight modifications, ActiveButtons could be incorporated into any program that requires the user to make selections which affect the direction the program takes.

Summary

This chapter has examined the essential aspects of controlling the Pascal Drawing window to set up the screen. It has also introduced some fundamental QuickDraw procedures from the Macintosh Toolbox to draw the input screen and use the mouse to control a program.

It can be seen from the previous examples that programming for the mouse requires as much programming of the screen as it does of the mouse. The programmer, therefore, must ensure that what is required of the user is clearly described on the screen.

2

Macintosh Graphics Concepts

Chapter 1 stated that graphics and mouse programming are intimately linked. Successful programming utilizing the mouse requires the programmer to be familiar with the ways in which the Macintosh handles and displays graphics. This chapter examines the drawing environment of the Macintosh in greater detail. In later chapters we will use this knowledge in some rather sophisticated programs. In order to understand Macintosh graphics concepts, you must be familiar with both the Boolean logical operations and the various numbering systems used by the Macintosh. To this end we have included Appendix B, which briefly explains and illustrates the tools required of all programmers who wish to delve inside the Macintosh.

Essential Macintosh Graphics Concepts

The basis for all graphics operations on the Macintosh are the routines grouped together under the collective name of *QuickDraw*. This chapter examines the concepts embodied in QuickDraw and discusses those features of the QuickDraw drawing environment that may be used by the programmer to control the Macintosh screen.

The Drawing Plane

The QuickDraw *drawing plane* may be thought of as a piece of paper with imaginary grid lines on it. As illustrated in Figure 2-1, the coordinate plane used by QuickDraw consists of a horizontal axis and a vertical axis. The two axes define a plane upon which there are 4,294,967,296 unique points. Each point appears at the intersection of a horizontal and vertical grid line. Because the grid lines are imaginary, they can be considered immeasurably thin. With respect

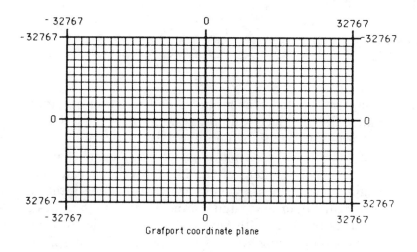

Figure 2-1. QuickDraw coordinate plane

to the Macintosh screen, they occur *between* the pixels. Thus, the grid lines are one pixel apart from one another. The horizontal and vertical coordinates range from −32767 to +32767. Coordinate values increase on the plane from left to right and from top to bottom. The origin (0,0) of the drawing plane is located in the middle of the grid.

All information passed to QuickDraw about the location, placement, or movement of the mouse pointer is in terms of coordinate points on the QuickDraw plane. The upper left corner of the Macintosh screen is associated with the coordinate (0,0). The screen displays the vertical grid lines 0 through 512 (the width of the screen) and the horizontal grid lines 0 through 342 (the height of the screen). Thus, the lower right corner of the Macintosh screen has the coordinates 512 and 342.

Points

Any *point* on the plane may be referenced in terms of its horizontal and vertical coordinates. Points can be stored in a Pascal variable of type Point, which is defined as

```
type    VHSelect = (V,H);
        Point     = record case integer of
                      0: (v:   integer;
                          h:   integer);
                      1: (vh:   array [VHSelect] of integer)
        end;
```

The point may be referenced as either a horizontal and vertical coordinate or as two elements in an array with the vertical coordinate followed by the horizontal coordinate. The pixel associated with the coordinate point hangs below and to the right of that point because the grid lines are immeasurably thin and, conceptually, lie in between the pixels.

Rectangles

A *rectangle* may be defined as any two points on the coordinate plane associated with the upper left and lower right corners of the rectangle.

Rectangles are used by QuickDraw to define active areas of the screen, map coordinate systems for graphics entities, and specify locations and sizes for QuickDraw drawing commands. QuickDraw provides routines to perform calculations on rectangles. These rectangles can be moved around the screen and the sizes changed. (The definition for the Rect data type was given in Chapter 1.)

Regions

On a larger scale, QuickDraw has the ability to gather an arbitrary set of points into a structure called a *region*. A region consists of the area contained within the set of points. For example, a rectangle is a special type of region having a predefined shape. A circle, triangle, or any other enclosed shape can be considered a region. Once the region has been defined, it is possible to perform many different calculations and graphics operations upon that region. The concept of regions is fundamental to QuickDraw and to the Macintosh user interface. Special QuickDraw routines are available to translate a set of points into the region structure. The region is a highly complex concept and will not be discussed further in this book.

Bit Images

While coordinate planes, points, rectangles, and regions are all good mathematical models, they do not have a physical appearance. Graphics entities that do have a physical appearance are those such as the bit image, bit map, pattern, and cursor.

A *bit image* is a rectangular collection of bits. Consider a row of bytes of any length. Now imagine several of these rows stacked one on top of another. You now have a matrix or rectangular array of bits that is a bit image. The number of bytes in a row is called the *row width* of that image. Bit images may be stored as any static or dynamic variable with any size of row width.

The Macintosh screen is *bit mapped*. Bit mapped screens use a special area of the computer's memory that contains a pixel-by-pixel representation of the screen. The bits comprising this area of memory are used by Macintosh to construct a screen image. Bits set to 0 in the screen memory produce a white pixel, while bits set to 1 produce a black pixel on the screen.

As you read earlier, the Macintosh screen contains 175,104 pixels. Each pixel corresponds to a single bit within the bit image representing the Macintosh screen. Since the screen is 342 pixels tall and 512 pixels wide, this results in a row width of 64 bytes in the bit image representing the screen.

Bit Maps

When the physical entity (a black or white dot) of a bit image is combined with the conceptual entities of the coordinate plane and the rectangle, the result is a *bit map*. Bit maps consist of three parts: a pointer to the bit image, the row width of that bit image, and a boundary rectangle that places a coordinate system on the bit image. It should be emphasized that a bit map does not actually contain the bits themselves, but only a pointer to them. Because of this, it is possible for several bit maps to point to the same bit image, each imposing a different coordinate system on it. The data structure of a bit map is defined in the Macintosh Toolbox as follows:

```
type    BitMap = record
                    baseAddr:   QDPtr;
                    rowBytes:   integer;
                    bounds:     Rect;
        end;
```

The baseAddr field locates the bit image in memory. In essence, this is the beginning of a set of bytes that defines the bit image. The rowBytes field contains the number of bytes in each row of the bit image. Because the Macintosh's microprocessor requires that memory be referenced by *words* (a word is equal to two bytes on the Macintosh) instead of individual bytes, both the baseAddr field and the rowBytes field should be even numbers.

The bounds field of the BitMap data type specifies a rectangle of active bits within the bit image. It is possible that some bits of a bit image may not be included in the bit map because they lie outside the rectangle that specifies the boundary of the bit map.

The boundary rectangle is used primarily to impose a coordinate system on the bit image. Here again, as on the Macintosh screen as a whole, the pixels in the image fall between points on the coordinate plane, so that the pixel associated with a point lies below and to the right of that point. In other words, if a bit is to be displayed at the coordinate (4,7), it will appear as a square bounded by the points (4,7) in the upper left corner and (5,8) in the lower right corner.

Bit images are convenient tools for generating and manipulating graphics entities through a single label (the pointer). QuickDraw utilizes the bit image to define several important graphics entities that make up part of the Macintosh's visual user interface. Among the most common and recognizable of these are patterns, cursors, and icons.

Patterns

Patterns are 64-bit images organized as 8-by-8 bit squares. They are used to define repeating images like tones or designs. The patterns in MacPaint are the most obvious example of QuickDraw patterns. They may be used to draw lines and shapes, or to fill areas of the screen. Patterns, when drawn, are aligned so that adjacent areas of the same pattern will blend into a continuous, coordinated pattern. QuickDraw provides several predefined patterns, including white, black, gray, light gray, and dark gray. Any 64-bit variable may also be used as a pattern. The data type for a pattern is the following:

```
type Pattern = packed array [0..7] of 0..255;
```

The row width of a pattern is 1 byte because it is an 8-by-8 bit square.

Cursors

By now you have probably become familiar with the *cursor*, the small picture that moves with the mouse. Movements of the cursor are related to the movements of the mouse. The cursor itself is not actually a part of the screen image. It has its own special software that is used to place the cursor on the screen and connect it to the mouse. As far as QuickDraw is concerned, a cursor is defined as a

256-bit image—a 16-by-16 bit square with the rowBytes field of the BitMap set to 2. Cursors are discussed in detail in Chapter 3.

Icons

Icons are 1024-bit images organized as a 32-by-32 bit square. The rowBytes field of an icon bit map is set to 4. QuickDraw contains several procedures for defining and manipulating icons. Icons are used on the desktop to represent things like files, folders, and applications.

Transfer Modes

The process of drawing lines, shapes, text, or any other type of image consists mainly of transferring one bit image to another. QuickDraw allows you to overlay a source image onto a destination image with varying effects, based upon the *transfer mode* in use. There are two kinds of transfer modes, depending upon what you are transferring:

1. The *pattern transfer mode* is used for drawing lines or shapes with a pattern.
2. The *source transfer mode* is used for drawing text or transferring any bit image between two bit maps.

You would use a pattern transfer to give an image a specific texture or color. On occasion you may want to change the pattern of a specific image, such as when a menu item becomes gray to signify that it is disabled. In this instance you would use the pattern transfer mode to specify how you want the new pattern to affect the pattern being displayed. In changing a menu item to gray, you would overlay a gray pattern using a pattern transfer that only affects the black pixels.

Now assume that you have a pie chart that you want to label. To write text on a shaded area, you would specify a source transfer mode to achieve a desired effect. In this instance you would want the characters to be on a solid background so that they could be read easily. This requires a source transfer mode that overwrites its destination (the characters being designed to have a solid background).

To achieve various overlaying effects, there are four basic transfer modes: Copy, OR, XOR, and Bic. The Copy mode simply replaces the pixels in the destination location with those in the source location, achieving a painting effect. The contents of the destination bit image have no effect on the final result.

The OR operation does not change the pixels under the white part of the source pattern. It changes only the pixels under the black parts of the source pattern. This effectively overlays the destination bit map with the source pattern. This is equivalent to performing the inclusive OR operation between the corresponding bits of the two images.

The XOR operation has no effect on the pixels under the white pixels of the source pattern, but it inverts the pixels under the black bits of the source pattern. This is equivalent to performing the exclusive OR operation between the corresponding bits of the two images.

The Bic operation has no effect on pixels under the white part of the source pattern. It forces the pixels under the black bits to become white.

Each of the basic transfer mode operations also has a variant, NOT, in which the source pattern is inverted before the operation is performed. Including NOT, there are eight transfer operations in all.

Figure 2-2 illustrates the different transfer mode operations. Table 2-1 shows the constants that may be used in Macintosh Pascal to refer to each operation.

Transfer mode names (such as patCopy, srcCopy, and patOr) are predefined constants under Macintosh Pascal. You would use the constants containing the characters "pat" to invoke a pattern transfer mode or the constants containing the characters "src" to invoke a source transfer mode.

GrafPorts

A *grafPort* is a complete drawing environment that defines how and where graphics operations will take place. It contains complete information about one particular environment and is kept separate from all other environments. All drawing, whatever its nature, takes place in a grafPort. Under normal circumstances, there is at least

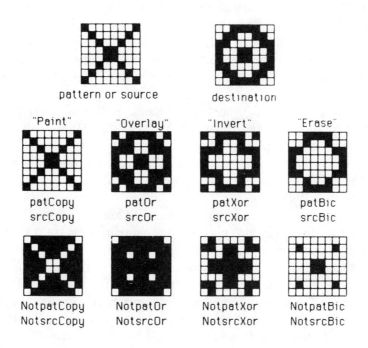

Figure 2-2. *Transfer mode operations*

Table 2-1. *Transfer Modes*

Pattern Transfer Mode	Source Transfer Mode	Action on Each Pixel in Destination:	
		Black Pixel in Pattern or Source	White Pixel in Pattern or Source
patCopy	srcCopy	Force black	Force white
patOr	srcOr	Force black	Leave alone
patXor	srcXor	Invert	Leave alone
patBic	srcBic	Force white	Leave alone
notpatCopy	notsrcCopy	Force white	Force black
notpatOr	notsrcOr	Leave alone	Force black
notpatXor	notsrcXor	Leave alone	Invert
notpatBic	notsrcBic	Leave alone	Force White

one grafPort associated with every visible window on the Macintosh screen. Through this grafPort, characters and graphics are drawn in the window. More than one grafPort may be associated with a window that can give the impression of a split screen. GrafPorts can be quite complex and will not be used in any of the examples in this book. However, a grafPort does provide some very important concepts that need to be understood before the topic of windows is covered.

One of the most important concepts is the imposition of a coordinate plane upon the drawing surface. The Macintosh screen has a special grafPort associated with it that places a *global coordinate system* on the screen in general. These coordinates have already been discussed—the upper left corner is point (0,0) and the lower right corner is (342,512).

Because each window must have at least one grafPort associated with it, each window may have a coordinate system that applies to that window only. This coordinate system is called the *local coordinate system*, and it is measured relative to the upper left corner of the window, not the upper left corner of the screen. For example, suppose there is a window with its upper left corner placed at global coordinate (50,50). If you were to draw a point at local coordinate (15,15), then that same point could also be drawn at global coordinate (65,65). Routines are available within QuickDraw that convert from other local grafPort coordinate systems into the global coordinate system.

Although each window with its own grafPort also has its own local coordinate system, all windows on the screen share the same global coordinate system. Coordinate systems and windows are discussed in greater depth in Chapter 5.

A grafPort is defined by a dynamic data structure that has the following format:

```
grafPort = record

        device:        integer;
        portBits:      BitMap;
        portRect:      Rect;
        visRgn:        RgnHandle;
        clipRgn:       RgnHandle;
        bkPat:         Pattern;
        fillPat:       Pattern;
        pnLoc:         Point;
        pnSize:        Point;
        pnMode:        integer;
```

pnPat:	Pattern;
pnVis:	integer;
txFont:	integer;
txFace:	Style;
txMode:	integer;
txSize:	integer;
spExtra:	integer;
fgColor:	longInt;
bkColor:	longInt;
colrBit:	integer;
patStretch:	integer;
picSave:	QDHandle;
rgnSave:	QDHandle;
polySave:	QDHandle;
grafProcs:	QDProcsPtr;

It is beyond the scope of this book to describe the operation and use of all fields that make up the grafPort. Many of the fields are used by Macintosh's system software to maintain the screen itself. However, those fields that are important to drawing graphics on the screen will be explained in detail.

The first five fields of the grafPort record are used by the system to control the appearance of windows on the Macintosh screen. The next two fields, bkPat and fillPat, are patterns employed when QuickDraw is used either to fill an area of the screen with a pattern or to erase an area of the screen. Specifically, bkPat is used by the QuickDraw erase commands to replace whatever is being erased. FillPat is used by QuickDraw's fill commands to fill an area of the screen with a specific pattern.

The next five fields determine the characteristics of the graphics pen, and the following five fields determine the characteristics of any text that may be drawn. The graphics pen and text drawing will be discussed in later sections.

The fgColor, bkColor, and colorBit fields all contain information related to drawing in color. It is not yet possible to draw in color on the Macintosh, but the inclusion of these fields is a promising indication of things to come.

The patStretch field is used during printer output operations. Its value should not under any circumstances be changed by an applications program.

The picSave, rgnSave, and polySave fields contain handles to pictures, regions, or polygons that may be under construction at any time. Under normal circumstances, they are not accessed directly by an applications program.

The final field in the grafPort record is used by advanced programmers for customizing QuickDraw operations and in other advanced and highly specialized ways. An applications program should not change the value of this field.

The Graphics Pen

Each grafPort contains one pen capable of drawing only within the confines of that grafPort. Each pen has five basic characteristics: location, size, drawing mode, drawing pattern, and visibility. These characteristics relate to the grafPort fields pnLoc, pnSize, pnMode, pnPat, and pnVis, respectively.

The *pen location* is the point at which the pen will begin to draw when it is next activated. It must be remembered that the pen location is a point on the drawing plane and not a pixel in the bit image. Therefore, the pen has greater mobility than can be demonstrated on a bit-by-bit basis. There are no restrictions on movement or placement of the pen.

The *pen size* defines the height and width of the pen. The default size is a 1-by-1 bit square. Width and height of the pen may range from (0,0) to (32767,32767). However, if either the pen height or width is less than 1, the pen will not draw on the screen.

The *pen pattern* is the pattern the pen uses to draw when activated. It may be thought of as the ink in the pen. The pattern will be aligned with the grafPort's coordinate system (the upper left corner of the pattern is aligned with the upper left corner of the grafPort).

The *pen mode* determines how the pen pattern is transferred to the grafPort and how it will affect what already exists in that particular position in the grafPort. This is essentially a Boolean operation and was described in detail earlier.

The *pen visibility* determines whether the pen is visible (in other words, whether or not it draws on the screen).

Text Characteristics

Each grafPort contains all of the characteristics that are necessary for the drawing of text within that grafPort. These characteristics are the text font, text face, text mode, size of the text, and amount of space between characters. These characteristics relate to the txFont, txFace, txMode, txSize, and spExtra fields of the grafPort record.

Individual character attributes must be introduced before the general text characteristics are discussed. Figure 2-3 shows the various attributes associated with the design of a single character and introduces some of the terminology related to character construction. These terms, although not widely used, are self-explanatory.

In the text characteristics, the text font field is the font number that identifies the character font to be used when drawing text. The following table lists the available fonts and their font numbers, along with predefined constants that may be used in Macintosh Pascal:

Font Number	Font	Constant Name
0	System Font	systemFont
1	Applications Font	applFont
2	New York	newYork
3	Geneva	geneva
4	Monaco	monaco
5	Venice	venice
6	London	london
7	Athens	athens
8	San Francisco	sanFran
9	Toronto	toronto

The system font is so designated because it is the font used by the Macintosh operating system for drawing menu titles, for example, and menu commands. It is usually the Chicago font.

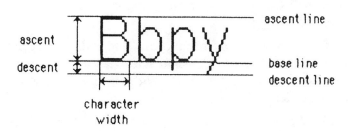

Figure 2-3. *Attributes in the design of a single character*

The applications font is really just a pointer to either New York or Geneva. This "font" is provided so that all applications programs that run on the Macintosh have a standard appearance. Characters in these fonts are proportionally spaced. This means that the letter "i," for example, does not require as much space as the letter "m."

A font is actually a collection of bit images. Each bit image contains a single character of the font. The font may consist of 256 distinct characters. Not all of these characters, however, may be defined. Each font contains a missing character symbol that is displayed if the character requested is not available within that font. This symbol usually takes the shape of a small square.

The text face determines the appearance of a font. All of the following effects are controlled by the txFace field of the grafPort: normal, bold, italic, underline, outline, shadow, condensed, and extended. These text faces may be applied alone or in combination. For example, a text face may be both boldface and italicized. The txFace field is of data type Style, which is defined as

```
type    StyleItem = (bold, italic, underline, outline,
                      shadow, condense, extend);
        Style     = set of StyleItem;
```

A summary of the effect of each of the StyleItem elements on text follows:

- **If txFace is set to bold,** each character is repeatedly drawn 1 bit to the right to add thickness. The number of repetitions used to boldface a character will vary, depending upon several of the other characteristics.

- **If txFace is set to italic,** character bits above the baseline are skewed to the right and bits below the baseline are skewed to the left.

- **If txFace is set to underline,** a line is drawn below the baseline of the characters. If a character has a descender like "p", the underline is not drawn through the pixel on either side of the descender.

- **If txFace is set to outline,** then the character is displayed as a hollow outline rather than as a solid figure.

- **If txFace is set to shadow,** not only is the character hollow and outlined, but the outline is thickened below and to the right of the character, thus achieving a shadow effect.

- **If txFace is set to condense,** the horizontal spacing between the characters is reduced.
- **If txFace is set to extend,** the horizontal spacing between the characters is increased.

The text mode determines how the characters of a font are transferred to the screen. It functions in much the same way as pen mode and was described in the section on transfer modes earlier in this book.

Text size determines the type size for the font in points. In Quick-Draw, a point equals 1/72nd of an inch (the size of one pixel) and any size may be specified. However, if the font is not available in that size, QuickDraw will rescale the available size. If this field is set to 0, the Font Manager will choose the size that is closest to the system font size (12 points).

The spExtra field is used to increase the horizontal distance between characters. It is usually used when a line of text needs to be fully justified (evenly spaced out across a given line width). The spExtra field contains the number of pixels that should be added to each character within the line.

Using New Fonts with QuickDraw

Unfortunately, although more fonts are becoming available to Macintosh owners by way of third party developers, it is not easy for programmers to use these fonts. When you become proficient at working with the outer levels of the Toolbox, you will be able to delve deeper into the Macintosh to access the font resource file.

Summary

This chapter has discussed the underlying concepts of drawing graphics on the Macintosh. The concepts of coordinate planes, points, and rectangles are an integral part of the operation of the functions used by QuickDraw. The graphics entities, bit images, and bit maps lead to the introduction of patterns, cursors, and icons. Boolean operations were shown to be essential to the transfer of graphics images between bit maps. These are important structures and concepts that will be used in upcoming programming examples.

The grafPort was introduced as the drawing environment. Many grafPort components were described, including the graphics pen and text drawing. The graphics pen determines where and how shapes and lines are drawn; it is also used in the positioning of text on the screen. QuickDraw gives a programmer great flexibility in the drawing of text in many different fonts, styles, and sizes.

The QuickDraw concepts and routines make it possible for the programmer to create visually appealing as well as informative program screens and displays.

3

Of Mice and Cursors

The cursor plays an important role in programming for the Macintosh. On the Macintosh desktop the cursor appears on the screen as an arrow, but in some applications programs, such as MacWrite and MacPaint, the cursor appears as a cross hair, a small hand, an I-beam, or a tiny wristwatch. The cursor is controlled by the mouse and lets the person using the Macintosh make selections based on the information presented on the screen. The Macintosh reads the position of the cursor on the screen and initiates actions when the user presses the mouse button. This chapter examines how cursors may be used in programs and how QuickDraw routines can be used to implement these methods.

Cursors, Cursors, Everywhere

The cursor itself is not actually a part of the screen image, although it is visible on the screen. It is a separate image placed on the screen by some of the routines in the Toolbox. It may be likened to a piece of cellophane placed over a piece of paper. The cellophane may have a picture on it that appears as part of the picture on the paper below, but the cellophane may be moved independently of the paper.

A cursor consists of two blocks of 32 bytes of memory. Each block is arranged as a 16-by-16 bit image with a point known as the *hotspot*. The Macintosh Pascal definition of a cursor is

```
type  Cursor = record
               data:     array [0..15] of integer;
               mask:     array [0..15] of integer;
               hotspot: Point;
      end;
```

As can be seen, one 16-by-16 bit image is known as the data and the other as the mask. Figure 3-1 shows how the data portion of the north-northwest arrow cursor is organized. By equating filled

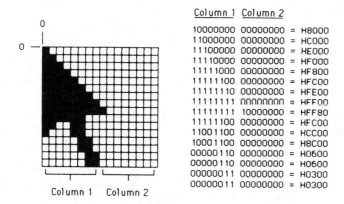

Figure 3-1. Organization of the data portion of an arrow cursor pointing north-northwest

squares with 1's, and empty squares with 0's, one can see how the image could be resolved into a stream of binary digits. This stream may be reduced even further by translating the bits into a hexadecimal number. Look at the arrow cursor in Figure 3-1. Column 1 represents the first byte of one line in the cursor and column 2 represents the second byte. Since each byte requires two hexadecimal digits, the resulting hexadecimal number is 4 digits long. This number is derived directly from converting the bits listed in the columns into a hexadecimal number.

The mask of a cursor determines how the cursor will appear on the screen. Each pixel (bit) in the screen, in the data block, and in the mask block is compared. The result of the comparison from the following table becomes the pixel on the screen.

Pixel in Mask	Pixel in Cursor	Resulting pixel On the screen
1	0	White
1	1	Black
0	0	Same as pixel under the cursor
0	1	Inverse of pixel under the cursor

The cursor may then be totally transparent or totally opaque, depending upon how the mask is set up. Figure 3-2 demonstrates the data image for a pointing finger and the mask that shows which

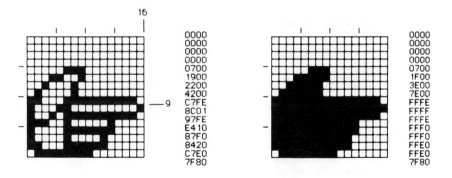

Figure 3-2. *Data image for a pointing finger and mask showing which parts of the cursor will be opaque and which parts transparent*

parts of the cursor will be opaque and which transparent.

The hotspot determines where the mouse is located on the screen according to the computer. Different cursors have their hotspots in different positions. The arrow has its hotspot at position (0,0), while the hotspot for the finger is position (16,9). The hotspot is used to align the cursor with the position of the mouse. When the position of the mouse is accessed in Macintosh Pascal, the point returned is the point at which the hotspot is located.

The Cursors Program

The following program demonstrates defining, moving, and using the cursor. Although the program is lengthy, its length is mostly due to overhead required by Pascal to define the image of the cursor using hexadecimal numbers.

Type the Cursors program into Macintosh Pascal. Save any previous program you might have on the screen and enter Cursors into the Untitled window. Because of the program's length, use the Save option frequently to save the program on disk. This lessens the chance of losing the entire program.

```
program Cursors;
  var
    Urect, SRect, XRect, TRect, FRect : Rect;
    SqCursor : Cursor;
    XCursor : Cursor;
    TextCursor : Cursor;
    FingCursor : Cursor;
  procedure SquareCurs;
    var
      Hot : Point;
      I : integer;
  begin
    SqCursor.Data[0] := $0000;
    SqCursor.Data[1] := $7FFE;
    for I := 2 to 13 do
      SqCursor.Data[I] := $4002;
    SqCursor.Data[14] := $7FFE;
    SqCursor.Data[15] := $0000;
    SqCursor.Mask[0] := 0;
    for I := 1 to 14 do
      SqCursor.Mask[I] := $7FFE;
    SqCursor.Mask[15] := 0;
    Hot.h := 1;
    Hot.v := 1;
```

```
  SqCursor.HotSpot := Hot;
end;
procedure CrossCurs;
 var
  Hot : Point;
  I : integer;
begin
 for I := 0 to 15 do
  XCursor.Data[I] := $0080;
 XCursor.Data[8] := $FFFF;
 for I := 0 to 15 do
  XCursor.Mask[I] := $0000;
 Hot.h := 8;
 Hot.v := 8;
 XCursor.HotSpot := Hot;
end;

procedure TextCurs;
 var
  Hot : Point;
  I : integer;
begin
 TextCursor.Data[0] := $0000;
 TextCursor.Data[1] := $0630;
 TextCursor.Data[2] := $0140;
 for I := 3 to 12 do
  TextCursor.Data[I] := $0080;
 TextCursor.Data[13] := $0140;
 TextCursor.Data[14] := $0630;
 TextCursor.Data[15] := $0000;

 for I := 0 to 15 do
  TextCursor.Mask[I] := 0;
 Hot.h := 12;
 Hot.v := 8;
 TextCursor.HotSpot := Hot;
end;
procedure FingerCurs;
 var
  Hot : Point;
  I : integer;
begin
 for I := 0 to 3 do
  FingCursor.Data[I] := $0000;
 FingCursor.Data[4] := $0700;
 FingCursor.Data[5] := $1900;
 FingCursor.Data[6] := $2200;
 FingCursor.Data[7] := $4200;
 FingCursor.Data[8] := $C7FE;
 FingCursor.Data[9] := $8C01;
 FingCursor.Data[10] := $97FE;
 FingCursor.Data[11] := $E410;
 FingCursor.Data[12] := $87F0;
```

```
FingCursor.Data[13] := $8420;
FingCursor.Data[14] := $C7E0;
FingCursor.Data[15] := $7F80;

for I := 0 to 3 do
  FingCursor.Mask[I] := 0;
FingCursor.Mask[4] := $0700;
FingCursor.Mask[5] := $1F00;
FingCursor.Mask[6] := $3E00;
FingCursor.Mask[7] := $7E00;
FingCursor.Mask[8] := $FFFE;
FingCursor.Mask[9] := $FFFF;
FingCursor.Mask[10] := $FFFE;
FingCursor.Mask[11] := $FFF0;
FingCursor.Mask[12] := $FFF0;
FingCursor.Mask[13] := $FFE0;
FingCursor.Mask[14] := $FFE0;
FingCursor.Mask[15] := $7F80;
Hot.h := 16;
Hot.v := 9;
FingCursor.HotSpot := Hot;
end;
procedure CursorControl;
 var
   MousePos : Point;
begin
 GetMouse(MousePos.h, MousePos.v);
 if PtInRect(MousePos, XRect) then
   SetCursor(XCursor)
 else if PtInRect(MousePos, TRect) then
   SetCursor(TextCursor)
 else if PtInRect(MousePos, SRect) then
   SetCursor(SqCursor)
 else if PtInRect(MousePos, FRect) then
   SetCursor(FingCursor)
 else
   InitCursor;
end;
procedure InitWindow;
 var
   Window : Rect;
begin
 HideAll;
 SetRect(Window, 0, 38, 511, 341);
 SetDrawingRect(Window);
 ShowDrawing;
end;
procedure TextInRect (Text : string;
         var r : Rect);
begin
   MoveTo((r.right - r.left - StringWidth(Text)) div 2 + r.left, (r.bottom - r.top) div 2 +
       r.top);
```

```
      DrawString(Text);
    end;
    procedure Setup;
    begin
     InitWindow;
     SetRect(Urect, 0, 0, 200, 120);
     PenNormal;
     PenSize(2, 2);
     OffsetRect(URect, 20, 15);
     FrameRect(URect);
     TRect := URect;
     TextInRect('Text Cursor Here', TRect);
     OffsetRect(URect, 256, 0);
     FrameRect(URect);
     SRect := URect;
     TextInRect('Square Cursor Here', SRect);
     OffsetRect(URect, 0, 150);
     FrameRect(URect);
     XRect := URect;
     TextInRect('Cross Cursor Here', URect);
     OffsetRect(URect, -256, 0);
     FrameRect(URect);
     FRect := URect;
     TextInRect('Finger Cursor Here', FRect);
     CrossCurs;
     SquareCurs;
     TextCurs;
     FingerCurs;
    end;
   begin
    SetUp;
    while not Button do
     CursorControl;
   end.
```

The Cursors program demonstrates the use of several cursors and the technique of changing the cursor, depending upon the cursor location on the screen. The program shows how to initialize four cursors — the finger cursor already mentioned, a text cursor, a cross cursor, and a square cursor.

Designing a Cursor

Before you attempt to program a cursor, get some graph paper and draw out the shape of the desired cursor. Figure 3-3 demonstrates how to draw the cross cursor. Using an area of the graph paper that

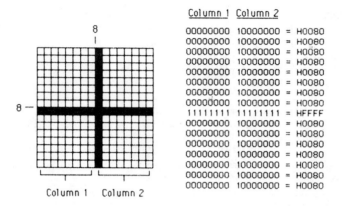

Figure 3-3. *Technique for designing a cross cursor*

is 16 squares wide by 16 squares high, fill in the squares that will be used to form the cross of the cursor. Once this is done, the image of the cursor must be converted into binary form. This is done by taking each square in succession, from left to right and top to bottom, and encoding it as a binary digit. If the square is blank, it becomes 0. If the square has been filled in, it becomes 1. Figure 3-3 shows the encoded binary digits to the right of the graphed representation of the cursor.

We now have a string of 256 bits that represents our cursor. To simplify the use of this data in a program, you should convert the binary digits to hexadecimal. For your convenience, Table 3-1 gives the conversions from binary to hexadecimal as well as from binary to decimal.

To use Table 3-1, divide your binary data into groups of four bits. Next write down the corresponding hexadecimal digit. When you reach the end of one row of bits, start a new hexadecimal number.

After the binary digits have been encoded into hexadecimal, it is possible to program the cursor as the Cursors program demonstrates. Figures 3-4 and 3-5 show the graphics and hexadecimal representations of the text cursor and the square cursor, respectively.

Masks are set up in exactly same way, resulting in a similar string of 64 hexadecimal digits.

Table 3-1. Conversion Table

Binary	Hexadecimal	Decimal
0000	0	0
0001	1	1
0010	2	2
0011	3	3
0100	4	4
0101	5	5
0110	6	6
0111	7	7
1000	8	8
1001	9	9
1010	A	10
1011	B	11
1100	C	12
1101	D	13
1110	E	14
1111	F	15

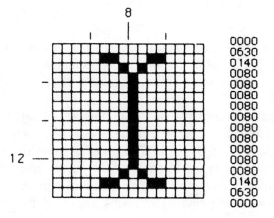

Figure 3-4. Graphics and hexadecimal representation of the text cursor

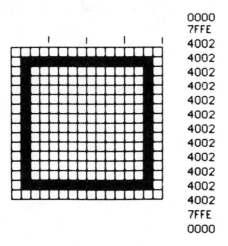

0000
7FFE
4002
4002
4002
4002
4002
4002
4002
4002
4002
4002
4002
4002
4002
7FFE
0000

Figure 3-5. *Graphics and hexadecimal representation of the*
square cursor

How the Cursors Program Works

Moving the mouse around causes the cursor to change as it enters the various rectangles on the screen. Each rectangle is labeled to show which cursor will appear in that rectangle. Here's how it works:

Initialization of the program consists of setting up the screen and initializing the cursors to be used. The procedures SquareCurs, CrossCurs, TextCurs, and FingerCurs use the hexadecimal strings that were constructed to define the cursor data and the cursor mask. This data is assigned to a variable of type cursor whose structure was discussed previously. Loops are used in some cases where the strings may repeat themselves.

The already familiar procedure InitWindow is used to initialize the Macintosh Pascal Drawing window. The four rectangles are drawn on the screen using the OffsetRect and FrameRect procedures. The TextInRect procedure centers any text string in any rectangle. TextInRect uses the QuickDraw function StringWidth to determine the length of the string that will be drawn on the screen. StringWidth is defined as

function StringWidth (s:Str255):integer;

where s is the string whose width will be measured by the function. The StringWidth function returns the width of the string in pixels.

The TextInRect procedure uses this information to calculate the string's horizontal starting position or indentation with respect to the left edge of the rectangle. The algebraic formula for the calculation is

Indentation = (Width of rectangle − Width of string)/2

The width of the rectangle is determined by subtracting the left coordinate from the right coordinate. The string width comes from the StringWidth function. The vertical center of the rectangle is similarly calculated, except that the string height is ignored. The MoveTo procedure is used to start the string at the indentation point from the left edge and at the center of the rectangle.

Once the initialization is complete, the program repeatedly passes control to the CursorControl procedure until the mouse button is pressed. Pressing the mouse button ends the program.

Each pass of the CursorControl procedure causes the program to retrieve the current position of the mouse using the GetMouse procedure. The current mouse position is evaluated to determine whether or not the cursor is located within one of the four rectangles. If the cursor is not located in any of the rectangles, the cursor will be set to the north-northwest arrow by the InitCursor statement.

If the cursor is moved into any one of the rectangles, the appropriate cursor is set through the use of the SetCursor procedure. The SetCursor procedure is defined as

procedure SetCursor (crsr:Cursor);

The variable *crsr* contains the cursor data, mask, and hotspot, information initialized by the appropriate procedure. The SetCursor procedure changes the current cursor to the cursor defined in crsr. If the cursor is visible on the screen, the change takes place immediately.

As you move the mouse around while running the program, visualize the statements that are executing the program, or try "stepping" through the program to understand just what is happening on the screen and in the program. This kind of cursor behavior is found in all Macintosh applications. Pay special attention to the parts of the screen that cause the cursor to change shape. In the Cursors program, it is the rectangles. In a program like MacPaint, it is the movement of the cursor in and out of the tool palette.

Summary

This chapter introduced the concept of cursor control and showed its application and use. It also demonstrated the design and coding of different cursor shapes, introduced the hotspot and described its application as the position of the mouse, and explained how the cursor indicates the effect of moving the mouse.

Cursors play an important role in the interaction between user and computer. Different cursors are used to inform the user of the current operation or state of a program. The hotspot of the cursor is the target that the Macintosh uses to determine cursor position, both during the drawing of the cursor, to align it, and during a mouse event that returns the position of the cursor to the program.

C H A P T E R

4

The Icon Editor

You probably recognize some or all of the symbols in Figure 4-1. They are called *icons* and are used by the Macintosh to represent different types of files on the Macintosh desktop. An icon is a set of black and white pixels that forms a picture that lets the user visually identify a document file, applications program, or another desktop item on the Macintosh. Some icons represent specialized functions; one such icon is the trash can, which is used for removing unwanted files from a disk. Icons are central to the Macintosh because they represent the way a user communicates with the computer. For example, MacWrite uses an icon that looks like a page with lines of text on it. The idea is to identify the file with word processing and written documents. Because icons are central to the Macintosh, Macintosh Pascal and QuickDraw have special procedures to create and use icons. This chapter illustrates how to take full advantage of these procedures.

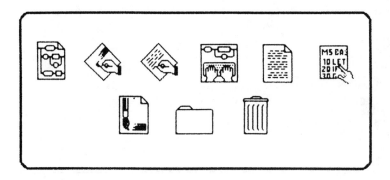

Figure 4-1. *Sample Macintosh icons*

Icons

Technically, an icon is a block of memory 128 bytes long. It is manipulated in much the same way as the cursor, in that the binary numbers contained in the memory block represent pixels on the screen. Figures 4-2 and 4-3 show two common icons. Icons and cursors have a lot in common, and it is frequently useful to think of the two as representing similar programming tasks. As you can see from Figures 4-2 and 4-3, there are more squares on the side of an icon than there are on the cursor. There are 32 squares on each side of the icon grid (whereas cursors are 16 pixels square). On the right side of each grid you will see two columns of hexadecimal numbers. These numbers make up the encoded bit patterns defining the icon. They comprise the code that would be set up in an array.

The IconEditor Program

Here is the complete listing of a program called the IconEditor. Although the program is rather long, it contains elements that will be used in later applications. Because the IconEditor program does not lend itself well to separation into distinct parts, we will discuss

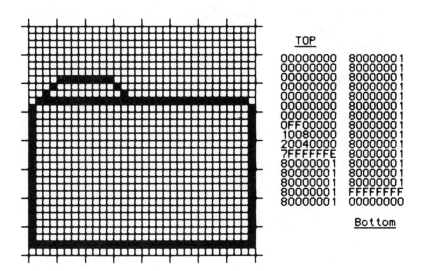

Figure 4-2.   Folder icon

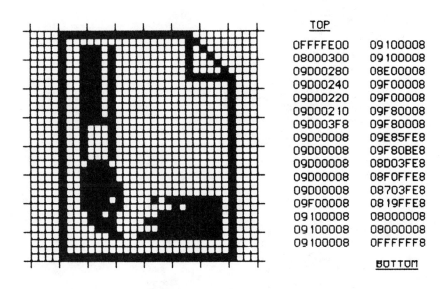

Figure 4-3.   MacPaint document icon

its construction and purpose after the program listing.

Enter this program into Macintosh Pascal. Pay special attention to detail. Because this is a long program, it's a good idea to save the program every ten or fifteen minutes using the Save option of the File menu.

```
program IconEditor;
 const
   SquareSize = 8;
   LeftBorder = 28;
   TopBorder = 46;
   PixelsInRect = 7;
 type
   IconBits = array[0..127] of char;
 var
   I, J : integer;
   Pencil : Cursor;
   EditArea, QuitButton, IconRect : Rect;
   MousePos : Point;
   WorkIconBits : IconBits;
   WorkIconPtr : QDPtr;
   WorkIcon : QDHandle;
   Mask : array[1..8] of integer;
 procedure InitWindow;
  var
    window : Rect;
 begin
   HideAll;
   SetRect(Window, 0, 0, 540, 370);
   SetDrawingRect(Window);
   ShowDrawing;
 end;
 procedure InitPencilCursor;
 begin
   Pencil.data[0] := $000E;
   Pencil.data[1] := $0009;
   Pencil.data[2] := $0011;
   Pencil.data[3] := $0018;
   Pencil.data[4] := $0026;
   Pencil.data[5] := $0024;
   Pencil.data[6] := $0044;
   Pencil.data[7] := $0048;
   Pencil.data[8] := $0088;
   Pencil.data[9] := $0090;
   Pencil.data[10] := $0110;
   Pencil.data[11] := $0120;
   Pencil.data[12] := $01C0;
   Pencil.data[13] := $0180;
   Pencil.data[14] := $0180;
   Pencil.data[15] := $0100;
```

```
Pencil.mask[0] := $000E;
Pencil.mask[1] := $000F;
Pencil.mask[2] := $001F;
Pencil.mask[3] := $001E;
Pencil.mask[4] := $003E;
Pencil.mask[5] := $003C;
Pencil.mask[6] := $007C;
Pencil.mask[7] := $0078;
Pencil.mask[8] := $00F8;
Pencil.mask[9] := $00F0;
Pencil.mask[10] := $01F0;
Pencil.mask[11] := $01E0;
Pencil.mask[12] := $01C0;
Pencil.mask[13] := $0180;
Pencil.mask[14] := $0180;
Pencil.mask[15] := $0100;

Pencil.hotSpot.h := 7;
Pencil.hotSpot.v := 16;
end;
procedure DrawGrid;
  var
    I, J : integer;
begin
  for I := 0 to 8 do
    begin
      MoveTo(20, 45 + I * 32); {Draw Horizontal Lines}
      Line(271, 0);
      MoveTo(27 + I * 32, 38); {Draw Vertical Lines}
      Line(0, 271);
      if I <> 8 then
        for J := 1 to 3 do
          begin
            MoveTo(27, 45 + I * 32 + J * 8);
            Line(256, 0);
            MoveTo(27 + I * 32 + J * 8, 45);
            Line(0, 256);
          end;
    end;
  SetRect(EditArea, 28, 46, 285, 303)
end;
procedure TextInRect (Text : string;
          var r : Rect);
  var
    FontRec : FontInfo;
    Height, Width : integer;
    PenStart : Point;
begin
  GetFontInfo(FontRec);
  Height := FontRec.ascent + FontRec.descent;
  Width := StringWidth(Text);
  PenStart.h := (r.right - r.left - Width) div 2 + r.left;
```

```
    PenStart.v := (r.bottom - r.top - Height) div 2 + r.top + FontRec.ascent;
    MoveTo(PenStart.h, PenStart.v);
    DrawString(Text);
  end;
  procedure InitMenu;
  begin
    SetRect(QuitButton, 350, 210, 420, 250);
    Pensize(2, 2);
    FrameRoundRect(QuitButton, 8, 8);
    TextInRect('Quit', QuitButton);
  end;
  procedure SetUp;
    var
      I : integer;
  begin
    ObscureCursor;
    PenNormal;
    InitWindow;
    DrawGrid;
    InitPencilCursor;
    InitMenu;
    Mask[1] := 128;
    for I := 2 to 8 do
      Mask[I] := Mask[I - 1] div 2;
    WorkIconPtr := @WorkIconBits;
    WorkIcon := @WorkIconPtr;
    for I := 0 to 127 do
      WorkIconBits[I] := chr(0);
    SetRect(IconRect, 348, 58, 384, 94);
    FrameRect(IconRect);
    InsetRect(IconRect, 2, 2);
  end;
  procedure ProcessMask (var BitInArray : Point;
             Color : boolean);
    var
      CurrentMask, ByteInArray, BitInByte : integer;
  begin
    ByteInArray := (BitInArray.v * 4) + (BitInArray.h div 8);
    BitInByte := (BitInArray.h - ((BitInArray.h div 8) * 8)) + 1;
    CurrentMask := Ord(WorkIconBits[ByteInArray]);
    if color then
      CurrentMask := CurrentMask - Mask[BitInByte]
    else
      CurrentMask := CurrentMask + Mask[BitInByte];
    WorkIconBits[ByteInArray] := chr(CurrentMask);
  end;
  procedure Edit (EditSquare : Point;
             color : boolean);
    var
      PixelRect : Rect;
  begin
    PixelRect.left := EditSquare.h * SquareSize + LeftBorder;
    PixelRect.top := EditSquare.v * SquareSize + TopBorder;
```

```
  PixelRect.right := PixelRect.left + PixelsInRect;
  PixelRect.bottom := PixelRect.top + PixelsInRect;
  if GetPixel(PixelRect.left, PixelRect.top) = Color then
    begin
      InvertRect(PixelRect);
      ProcessMask(EditSquare, Color);
    end;
  PlotIcon(IconRect, WorkIcon);
end;
function GetSquare (MousePos : Point) : Point;
var
  SquarePos : Point;
begin
  SquarePos.v := (MousePos.v - TopBorder) div SquareSize;
  SquarePos.h := (MousePos.h - LeftBorder) div SquareSize;
  GetSquare := SquarePos;
end;
function GetColor (StartSquare : Point) : boolean;
begin
  GetColor := GetPixel(StartSquare.h * SquareSize + LeftBorder, StartSquare.v * SquareSize
      + TopBorder);
end;
procedure TrackMouse;
var
  Event : EventRecord;
  LastEdit : Point;
  Color, Balance : boolean;
begin
  repeat
    repeat
      GetMouse(MousePos.h, MousePos.v);
      if PtInRect(MousePos, EditArea) then
        SetCursor(Pencil)
      else
        InitCursor;
    until GetNextEvent(MDownMask, Event);

    if PtInRect(Event.where, EditArea) then
      begin
        Color := GetColor(GetSquare(Event.where));
        Edit(GetSquare(Event.where), color);
        LastEdit := GetSquare(Event.where);
        repeat
          GetMouse(MousePos.h, MousePos.v);
          if PtInRect(MousePos, EditArea) then
            begin
              SetCursor(Pencil);
              if not EqualPt(LastEdit, GetSquare(MousePos)) then
                begin
                  Edit(GetSquare(MousePos), Color);
                  LastEdit := GetSquare(MousePos);
                end
            end
        end
```

```
        else
          InitCursor;
       until GetNextEvent(MUpMask, Event);
      end
     else
       Balance := GetNextEvent(MUpMask, Event);
      until PtInRect(Event.where, QuitButton);
    end;
   begin
       SetUp;
       TrackMouse;
       hideall;
    end.
```

After entering and checking the program using the Check option in the Run menu, run the program by selecting Go in the Run menu. You will see a screen that looks like Figure 4-4. The grid on the right of the screen may be compared to the grids shown in previous figures. In fact, the IconEditor program is a computerized version of standard graph paper. On the right side of the screen you see two rectangles, one of which is labeled Quit, the other of which is blank. The rectangle labeled Quit lets you stop the program by moving the mouse pointer into the Quit button and then pressing the mouse button. The blank rectangle is a display area that shows a full-size representation of the icon you are creating with the IconEditor program. In this respect, the display area is like the small real-size viewing area in MacPaint that appears when you are using FatBits.

In moving the mouse around the screen, you will notice that when the mouse is located within the grid area, the cursor becomes a pencil. This grid area is known as the edit area. In order to draw in the edit area, move the cursor over the grid square and click (press and release) the mouse button. This places a black pixel within the edit area. And if you look at the previously blank display area, you see that one of the pixels located in the rectangle has also turned black. Pixels in the display area correspond directly with the pixels in the edit area.

Now move the mouse to the top line of the edit area, press the mouse button, and drag it downward through the grid. Move the mouse five or six squares and release the mouse button. This action, called *dragging*, causes all the squares that the mouse passes over to turn black, creating a black line through the grid. You should see a similar line located in the display area.

Unlike the IconEditor program, a complete icon editing program is able to store and retrieve icons from the disk. With a little work

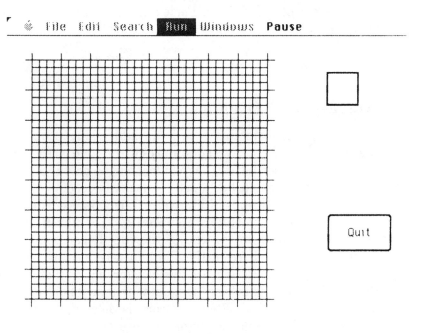

Figure 4-4. *The IconEditor screen*

this program could be made into a complete editor. The IconEditor does demonstrate the tools available for programming with the Macintosh mouse.

Inside the IconEditor

Though the IconEditor program is rather long, the purpose of its several parts is easily seen. However, there are problems in writing the IconEditor or a similar program that must be addressed by the programmer.

The first major problem is the difference between the screen representation of an icon in the edit area and the way in which an icon is actually stored in memory. A second problem is that of the program correctly interpreting the actions of the mouse. This question of interpretation is the most important in any program written to interact with the mouse. Both the effect of time and previous actions must be considered. For example, what will be the effect of clicking on a square that is already black?

Addressing and Events

The first problem in this case is an addressing problem. Isolating the position of the activated square of the grid area relative to an origin at the upper left of the grid locates the actual byte in memory. To get at the affected bit, a set of masks is used.

The second problem is circumvented by a device called the *Macintosh event queue*. A queue is a special type of file in which records are always written to the end of the file. Records may be read or deleted from anywhere in the file, but a request to read a specific type of record will return the first occurrence of that record type in the file. Note that this "file" is a data structure held in memory and not a file on the disk. When a record is deleted, the next record of the same type becomes available for use by a program.

The event queue is maintained by the Macintosh Toolbox. As different events occur, an event record is added to the end of the event queue. An event record has the following structure:

```
type  EventRecord = record
                    what:      integer; {event number}
                    message:   longint;
                    when:      longint;
                    where:     Point;
                    modifiers: integer;
      end;
```

The "what" field is a code known as the event number. It represents the kind of event that occurred—for example, the mouse button being pressed down.

The message field contains extra information that may be required to process the event. For example, the message field of event records that result from key presses on the keyboard contains information about which key was pressed.

The "when" field contains the system clock time of the event in ticks. A tick is one-sixtieth of a second. The tick field is set to zero when the Macintosh is first turned on.

The "where" field contains the mouse position at the time the event occurred.

The "modifiers" field is further divided into two fields. The first field indicates whether or not any special keys, such as the SHIFT key or OPTION key, were pressed at the time of the event. The second field indicates whether the mouse button was up or down.

Two functions are used to access the event queue—GetNextEvent and EventAvail. The two functions are very similar in application. The important difference between them is that GetNextEvent deletes the event record from the queue and EventAvail does not.

The two functions are defined as follows:

```
function GetNextEvent(eventMask:integer;
   var theEvent:EventRecord):boolean;


function EventAvail(eventMask:integer;
   var theEvent:EventRecord):boolean;
```

The variable eventMask contains a code that specifies which event type you want to be returned. The mask can be thought of as a filter that selects only those events that you want.

Both of the functions above yield False if there is no event of the requested type. If there is an event of the requested type, both functions return True and theEvent is filled with the requested event record.

Table 4-1 shows the event numbers, the applicable event mask, and a description of the event. It is possible to request the first event of a number of types by adding the masks together. For example, if you want the next mouse event, not caring whether it is a mouse button down or a mouse button up event, you could set the mask to the total of the masks for the two events. In this example, that value is six.

Table 4-2 shows the possible values of the modifier field of the event record. The modifier field assists in determining which event has occurred and if any peripheral keystrokes took place during the event. For example, the mask would indicate whether the mouse was clicked, but the modifier would tell you whether the OPTION key was pressed at the same time.

The modifier field determines the meaning of the modifier keys on the keyboard at the time the event is sent to the event queue. The codes in Table 4-2 determine which keys were held down at the time of the event. By using a mask in a manner similar to the way in

Table 4-1. *Event Numbers, Masks, and Descriptions*

Event Number	Event Mask	Event Description
0	1	Null Event
1	2	Mouse Button Depressed
2	4	Mouse Button Released
3	8	Key Depressed
4	16	Key Released
5	32	Auto Key
6	64	Update Event
7	128	Disk Inserted
8	256	Activate Deactivate Event
9	512	Abort Event
10	1024	Network Event
11	2048	I/O Driver Event
12	4096	Applications Event 1
13	8192	Applications Event 2
14	16384	Applications Event 3
15	−32768	Applications Event 4

Table 4-2. *Modifier Field Values*

Code	Meaning
0	Deactivate
1	Activate
2	Applications Window
128	Mouse Button Depressed
256	COMMAND Key
512	SHIFT Key
1024	CAPS LOCK Key
2048	OPTION Key

which masks are used for the "what" field, it is possible to determine which keys are held down.

Codes 0, 1, and 2 are used for special events connected with the Window Manager. They are described in the advanced programming section later in this book.

The modifier field may be used in connection with a mouse button up event, in which case a modifier key alters the effect of a mouse action. An example of this occurs in the MacPaint program. When you use the lasso to move an object around the screen, the OPTION key modifies the effect of the mouse by duplicating the object held by the lasso.

The event queue allows programmers to control how different events are processed, even though programmers do not have control over the events themselves.

Clicking and Dragging

In the IconEditor program, we are using two separate mouse actions—a click and a drag. While these are two separate actions, both commence with the same mouse button down event. When the mouse button is depressed, the program must determine whether it is the start of a click or the start of a drag. The difference between a click and a drag is one of movement. The results of either action are, however, the same for the initial pixel square on the grid. At the time of the mouse button down event, the square at which the cursor is located will be inverted (black turning white and white turning black) whether or not the action is a click or continues as a drag.

Once the initialization of the program is complete, the IconEditor program will be in one of two states. It is either waiting for a mouse action or processing a mouse action. The action can take the form of a mouse button down or mouse button up movement, or any combination of these events. While waiting for a mouse action, the program monitors the position of the cursor and checks that the correct cursor is being displayed to the user on the screen. After an action has been initiated by a mouse button down event, if the event occurred within the grid edit area, the initial square under the cursor is edited. If movement then becomes apparent, successive squares are edited as the cursor is dragged across the edit area. A mouse button up event terminates the action and the program returns to the wait state.

The Body of the IconEditor Program

The IconEditor program consists of two main procedures—the SetUp procedure and the TrackMouse procedure. SetUp initializes the program as it draws the screen, sets the cursors, and sets the variables. The TrackMouse procedure is the basis both for maintaining the correct cursor and for performing the actual editing.

```
procedure SetUp;
 var
  I : integer;
begin
 ObscureCursor;
 PenNormal;
 InitWindow;
 DrawGrid;
 InitPencilCursor;
 InitMenu;
 Mask[I] := 128;
 for I := 2 to 8 do
  Mask[I] := Mask[I - 1] div 2;
 WorkIconPtr := @WorkIconBits;
 WorkIcon := @WorkIconPtr;
 for I := 0 to 127 do
  WorkIconBits[I] := chr(0);
 SetRect(IconRect, 348, 58, 384, 94);
 FrameRect(IconRect);
 InsetRect(IconRect, 2, 2);
 end;
```

The SetUp procedure used in the IconEditor program commences when you use the built-in Toolbox ObscureCursor procedure to hide the cursor while the screen is drawn. The ObscureCursor procedure helps hide the cursor when it is not in use. This indicates to the program user that the program is not yet ready for processing. An example of the use of ObscureCursor is in the MacWrite program. MacWrite hides the cursor when a user is typing into the document window. When the mouse is moved, the cursor immediately reappears on the screen, allowing the user to edit or select with the mouse as usual. ObscureCursor needs no definition in Macintosh Pascal and can be thought of as an intrinsic procedure.

The PenNormal procedure initializes both the pen and the window. The window is set large enough so that it encompasses the entire screen without the boundaries of the window being visible. As both of these procedures have been used earlier in this book, you should be familiar with them by now.

Creating the IconEditor Grid

The following listing will create the IconEditor grid:

```
procedure DrawGrid;
  var
    I, J : integer;
begin
  for I := 0 to 8 do
    begin
    MoveTo(20, 45 + I * 32); {Draw Horizontal Lines}
    Line(271, 0);
    MoveTo(27 + I * 32, 38); {Draw Vertical Lines}
    Line(0, 271);
    if I <> 8 then
      for J := 1 to 3 do
        begin
        MoveTo(27, 45 + I * 32 + J * 8);
        Line(256, 0);
        MoveTo(27 + I * 32 + J * 8, 45);
        Line(0, 256);
      end;
    end;
  SetRect(EditArea, 28, 46, 285, 303)
end;
```

After the pen has been initialized by the SetUp procedure, it is possible to draw the editing grid on the screen. The DrawGrid procedure draws the grid lines that appear on the left side of the screen. There are two loops in this procedure. The main loop draws the lines that project outside the edit area, and an inner loop draws the lines in between. Both horizontal and vertical lines are drawn within the same pass of the loop. The lines are drawn using the MoveTo and Line procedures. The MoveTo procedure has the effect of moving the graphics pen to whatever position is defined by its parameter list. As we have seen, it is defined as

procedure MoveTo (h, v:integer);

where h is the horizontal component and v is the vertical component of the point on the drawing plane.

The procedure Line is defined as

procedure Line (dh, dv:integer);

where *dh* specifies the horizontal distance of the line and *dv* specifies
the vertical distance of the line. Thus, the Line procedure will connect the current pen position to a point that is dh pixels left or right
(depending upon whether a positive or negative value is given) and
dv pixels up or down.

In the IconEditor program, each component of the point is calculated as the loop progresses. The outer loop draws the extended lines
(the lines that stick out from the grid). There are three standard-size
lines between each extended line drawn by the inner loop. The loop
control variables are used to position the lines relative to the top and
left borders. The extended lines are 32 pixels apart (as indicated by
the multiplication in the MoveTo parameter list), and the standard
lines are 8 pixels apart (after being set in relationship to the nearest
extended line—hence the multiplication by 32 and then by 8). The top
border for the extended lines is 38 and the top border for the standard lines is 46. The left border is 20 for the extended lines and 28 for
the standard lines. When the outer loop is complete, the SetRect
procedure is used to set the size of the EditArea variable. The
DrawGrid procedure then returns control to the SetUp procedure.

The SetUp procedure continues by initializing the pencil cursor
through InitPencilCursor. This procedure is similar to the cursor
procedures investigated in Chapter 3.

```
procedure InitMenu;
begin
   SetRect(QuitButton, 350, 210, 420, 250);
   Pensize(2, 2);
   FrameRoundRect(QuitButton, 8, 8);
   TextInRect('Quit', QuitButton);
end;
```

After the cursor initialization, the InitMenu procedure is invoked
to draw the Quit button. The Quit button terminates the program
when clicked on. The InitMenu procedure uses a version of the Text-
InRect procedure slightly different from the one used earlier. The
major difference between this TextInRect procedure and the procedure demonstrated earlier in the book is the TextInRect procedure's
ability to determine the height of the text itself before centering it

within the rectangle. This is accomplished by using the QuickDraw procedure GetFontInfo, which is defined as

procedure GetFontInfo (var info:FontInfo);

The GetFontInfo procedure returns information about the font currently in use within the grafPort. It takes into consideration any variations of style and size currently in effect. Within the record FontInfo, the following information is returned: the height of the character above the baseline, the height of the character below the baseline, the maximum width of the character, and the total height of the character. These characteristics were described in detail in Chapter 2.

The TextInRect procedure gets the FontInfo record to determine both the height of the character and the location of the baseline. This information is used to correctly center the text within the specified rectangle. Both the height and width of the text are taken into account.

At this point in the SetUp procedure, the masks for bit manipulation are set. The mask array holds a value corresponding to a particular bit within the byte. Mask[1] corresponds to the high-order bit and therefore has the value of 128. Each succeeding bit has a value of one-half that of the preceding bit. Thus, the seven passes of the loop generate the necessary values corresponding to each bit in the byte.

The next two statements of SetUp initialize the pointer and the handle to the array that contains the icon to be edited. The array is then cleared through the use of the loop.

The remainder of SetUp draws the frame around the location where the real-size icon appears on the screen. This is done by using the SetRect procedure to delimit the size and position of the frame and by using the FrameRect procedure to draw it. The frame is 4 pixels larger in each direction than the icon itself. Therefore, it is necessary to shrink the rectangle that has been specified by 4 pixels in order to arrive at a rectangle in which the icon will be displayed. The InsetRect procedure performs this function. It is defined as

procedure InsetRect (var r:Rect; dh, dv:integer);

The InsetRect procedure is one of QuickDraw's calculation procedures. It shrinks or expands a rectangle by the values contained in the parameters dh and dv. If the values contained by these parameters are positive, the rectangle is shrunk by the amounts specified. Otherwise, the rectangle is expanded by these values.

With the IconEditor program, it is necessary to shrink the rectangle by 4 pixels in each direction. For that reason, a value of 2 is used for each parameter. Each edge is moved inward by 2 pixels, giving the total of the 4 required pixels. This completes the initialization of the program.

Editing with the IconEditor Program

The second main procedure of the IconEditor program is the TrackMouse procedure.

```
procedure TrackMouse;
 var
   Event : EventRecord;
   LastEdit : Point;
   Color, Balance : boolean;
begin
 repeat
  repeat
   GetMouse(MousePos.h, MousePos.v);
   if PtInRect(MousePos, EditArea) then
    SetCursor(Pencil)
   else
    InitCursor;
  until GetNextEvent(MDownMask, Event);

  if PtInRect(Event.where, EditArea) then
  begin
   Color := GetColor(GetSquare(Event.where));
   Edit(GetSquare(Event.where), color);
   LastEdit := GetSquare(Event.where);
   repeat
    GetMouse(MousePos.h, MousePos.v);
    if PtInRect(MousePos, EditArea) then
     begin
      SetCursor(Pencil);
      if not EqualPt(LastEdit, GetSquare(MousePos)) then
       begin
        Edit(GetSquare(MousePos), Color);
        LastEdit := GetSquare(MousePos);
       end
     end
  end
```

```
    else
      InitCursor;
    until GetNextEvent(MUpMask, Event);
  end
  else
    Balance := GetNextEvent(MUpMask, Event);
  until PtInRect(Event.where, QuitButton);
end;
```

Once the program is initialized, the TrackMouse procedure takes control. As with the cursor demonstration program from Chapter 3, the first loop of the TrackMouse procedure maintains the correct cursor depending upon the position of the mouse. If the mouse is within the grid edit area, the pencil cursor is displayed; otherwise the arrow cursor is used. This loop repeats until a mouse button down event occurs. If the mouse button down event occurs within the Quit button, the program terminates. If the mouse button down event occurs outside of the edit area and outside of the Quit button, the program ignores the event and goes back to maintaining the cursor. It is when the mouse button down event occurs inside of the edit area that editing (drawing black or white pixels) takes place.

There are two phases to editing because the mouse button down event may signal either the beginning of a click or the beginning of a drag. The difference between the two actions is one of movement from square to square on the grid. After the mouse button down event has occurred, an immediate edit takes place for the square in which the event occurred. The procedure then looks for movement to another square. If movement does occur, successive edits are initiated. The edit on the initial square dictates the edit for all later squares. For example, if the initial edit turns the first square from black to white, successive movement across other squares will also turn them to white. This emulates the FatBits option of MacPaint.

The first action taken by the program after the mouse button down event occurs is to determine the color of the initial square. To do this, the GetSquare function is invoked to determine the actual square in which the mouse button down event occurred. This function determines the square of any mouse point by subtracting the associated borders of the edit area from the corresponding component of the mouse position. The result is then divided by 8 to resolve screen pixels into grid edit squares.

The GetColor function is used to obtain the color of a square. The GetColor function determines the location of the pixel in the upper left corner of the edit square; it then uses the GetPixel function to determine whether that pixel is black or white. The GetPixel function is a QuickDraw function that is defined as

function GetPixel (h, v:integer):boolean;

This function returns True if the pixel specified by *h* and *v* is black or False if it is white.

The Edit Procedure

When the color of the initial square has been determined, then that square is edited to set its color. This is done by passing the edit square and the color to the Edit procedure.

```
procedure Edit (EditSquare : Point;
          color : boolean);
  var
    PixelRect : Rect;
begin
  PixelRect.left := EditSquare.h * SquareSize + LeftBorder;
  PixelRect.top := EditSquare.v * SquareSize + TopBorder;
  PixelRect.right := PixelRect.left + PixelsInRect;
  PixelRect.bottom := PixelRect.top + PixelsInRect;
  if GetPixel(PixelRect.left, PixelRect.top) = Color then
    begin
      InvertRect(PixelRect);
      ProcessMask(EditSquare, Color);
    end;
  PlotIcon(IconRect, WorkIcon);
end;
```

The Edit procedure calculates the rectangle that is encompassed by the edit square. It then determines whether or not the color of the square in question needs to be changed. This determination is made by determining the color of the square being edited and comparing it with the color of the original square. If the two are equal, then the square is changed by using the InvertRect procedure. The InvertRect procedure performs the color change of the square. The array containing the information that is used to plot the icon is now edited to alter the bit corresponding to the edited square. This function is accomplished by calling the ProcessMask procedure with the edit square and color as parameters.

```
procedure ProcessMask (var BitInArray : Point;
          Color : boolean);
   var
     CurrentMask, ByteInArray, BitInByte : integer;
begin
   ByteInArray := (BitInArray.v * 4) + (BitInArray.h div 8);
   BitInByte := (BitInArray.h - ((BitInArray.h div 8) * 8)) + 1;
   CurrentMask := Ord(WorkIconBits[ByteInArray]);
   if color then
     CurrentMask := CurrentMask - Mask[BitInByte]
   else
     CurrentMask := CurrentMask + Mask[BitInByte];
   WorkIconBits[ByteInArray] := chr(CurrentMask);
end;
```

The ProcessMask procedure calculates which byte in the array is affected by the square in question. It then determines the actual bit in the byte that needs to be changed. This byte is extracted from the array and the appropriate mask (depending upon the bit) is added to or subtracted from the current mask. The mask is then replaced into the array as a character using the Macintosh Pascal Chr function. Control is returned to the Edit procedure, which plots the icon using the PlotIcon procedure. The PlotIcon procedure is a Macintosh Pascal procedure defined as

procedure PlotIcon (theRect:Rect; theIcon:IconHandle);

This procedure plots the icon pointed to by *theIcon* on the screen at the position specified by *theRect*.

This completes processing of the edit procedure, and control is returned to the TrackMouse procedure. The position of the square that has just been edited is saved in the LastEdit variable. The program now looks for movement of the mouse. If the mouse moves from the original square edited to another square before a mouse button up event occurs, then the program assumes that a drag operation is in progress. The program continues to call the Edit procedure for each new square entered by the mouse as long as the mouse remains in the edit area and until the mouse button is released.

The program continues to track the mouse, editing when the appropriate mouse actions occur. The program terminates after a click occurs in the Quit button and control returns to the Macintosh Pascal interpreter.

Summary

This chapter showed how the Event Manager is used to track and control an application's use of mouse actions. The event queue was explained and its use in mouse programming shown.

The program IconEditor illustrated many of the techniques used to initialize and manipulate icons. It demonstrated the problems associated with relating a visible representation of internal events on the screen and showed how the connection between the two is made.

This chapter also illustrated the problems of distinguishing between different mouse actions that commence with the same event. Finally, the techniques used to solve these problems were discussed.

5

Primitive Window Management

Until now this book has used windows without thoroughly explaining them. Windows are the primary means of presenting information on the Macintosh and are therefore very important. They can be thought of as distinct work areas on the screen that are logically separated (within the computer's memory) from one another. Windows can be activated so that the task at hand takes place in one window. Other windows can be deactivated, made dormant on the desktop, while still other windows, including one active window, cover them. These dormant windows may then be activated by clicking them on with the mouse. Any number of windows may be open on the desktop, but there is only one active window at any time.

In the programs examined so far, windows and window manipulation have not been discussed in depth. In most of these programs, a single window was set so that it covered the entire screen. This chapter closely examines and details the techniques for window manipulation.

Macintosh Pascal and Window Manipulation

When you have Macintosh Pascal up and running, you may notice that each time you run a program you lose the ability to control the Pascal windows by directly using the mouse. While you are typing in or editing a program in Macintosh Pascal, the Pascal editor is in control of the computer. This editor lets you enter and edit text, manipulate windows, or select options from the pull-down menus. Once you run a program, however, you leave the Pascal editor, and the Macintosh is under control of the Pascal interpreter (which resides in memory) and the program being executed. Therefore, if you plan to manipulate windows while running a program in Pascal, you must write routines in your program that allow window manipulation.

Window Manipulation

Window manipulation refers to any actions that change the contents of a window, its size, or its position. Common window manipulations include moving a window by dragging from its title bar, resizing a window with the size box, scrolling through the contents of a window with the scroll bar, or entering and editing text within the window.

From the programmer's point of view, the anatomy of a window is important because a program must interpret certain mouse actions that affect a window. Figure 5-1 identifies the various parts of a window.

As seen in Figure 5-1, an average window consists of the active drawing area, the title bar, two scroll bars (one vertical and the other horizontal), and a size box. The active drawing area is the part

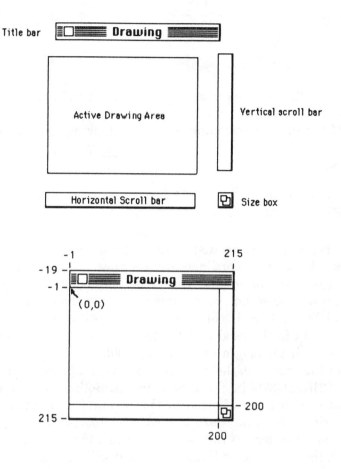

Figure 5-1. *Anatomy of a Macintosh window*

of the window in which drawing occurs. It is the size and position of this drawing area that is set by the SetDrawingRect procedure. The other components of the window are added by the Macintosh's Toolbox subsequent to the initialization of the drawing area by the Set-DrawingRect procedure.

A secondary coordinate plane takes effect when the drawing window has been set and is displayed upon the screen. Assume, for example, that you have set and displayed the drawing window with the following coordinates:

```
Top    = 150
Left   = 200
Bottom = 300
Right  = 350
```

The displayed window will be situated in the lower right corner of the screen.

If you draw a rectangle with the following coordinates.

```
Top    = 10
Left   = 10
Bottom = 20
Right  = 20
```

the rectangle will be displayed in the upper left corner of the window. A second coordinate plane now exists with its origin at (150,200), the upper left corner of the active drawing area of the window. This second coordinate plane introduces again the concepts of global and local coordinate systems. All drawing operations will now work in the local coordinate system (within the active drawing area) as if the origin were at (150,200).

In this example, the new rectangle would be drawn at the location (160,210,320,370) in global coordinates. Both drawing operations and mouse actions are affected by this second coordinate plane. Calls to the GetMouse procedure return coordinates in terms of the local origin. Therefore, if the mouse is above and to the left of the window, both the x and y coordinates returned will be negative. This relative relationship between coordinate planes is useful when dealing with grafPorts in different locations on the screen. Drawings within grafPorts will always be situated similarly within each grafPort regardless of where the grafPort is physically located on the screen.

It is important to note that the event queue is not affected by a window's position on the screen. The coordinates returned in the where field of the event record are always given in terms of the global coordinate system. To illustrate this, assume a drawing window has been set and displayed as follows:

```
Top    = 100
Left   = 100
Bottom = 200
Right  = 200
```

If the mouse is placed at the upper left of the active drawing area, a call to GetMouse returns (0,0) as the horizontal and vertical coordinates of the mouse. However, the "where" field in the event queue contains the coordinates (100,100) as the position of the mouse. This can cause a certain amount of confusion in programs that must locate both the global and local coordinates of the mouse.

The solution to this problem is to adjust one or the other of the mouse coordinates depending upon their use. If mouse position is required in terms of the window, then subtracting the window's origin from the where field of the event record returns the mouse's position in terms of the local coordinates. If the mouse's position is required in global coordinate terms, adding the window's origin to the results of a GetMouse operation results in a mouse position based on the global coordinate system.

The routines that control Window Manager functions of this type are only accessible by using the advanced features of the Macintosh Pascal interpreter. These features are discussed in Chapter 6.

The WindowManager Program

The following program illustrates various features of managing and manipulating windows. Carefully enter the program into Macintosh Pascal, remembering to save your typing frequently. Also use the Check option of the Run menu to check the syntax of your program each time you save. Checking longer programs in this way guarantees that each time you save your program you are saving a syntactically correct version.

```
program WindowManager;
  var
    MousePos, DeltaMouse : Point;
    Window, TitleBar, SizeBox, EditArea : Rect;
    MoveCursor, SizeCursor, SqCursor : Cursor;
  procedure SquareCurs;
    var
      I : integer;
  begin
    SqCursor.Data[0] := $0000;
    SqCursor.Data[1] := $7FFE;
    for I := 2 to 13 do
      SqCursor.Data[I] := $4002;
    SqCursor.Data[14] := $7FFE;
```

```
    SqCursor.Data[15] := $0000;
    SqCursor.Mask[0] := 0;
    for I := 1 to 14 do
      SqCursor.Mask[I] := $7FFE;
    SqCursor.Mask[15] := 0;
    SqCursor.HotSpot.h := 1;
    SqCursor.HotSpot.v := 1;
  end;
  procedure MoveCurs;
  begin
   MoveCursor.data[0] := $0000;
   MoveCursor.data[1] := $0000;
   MoveCursor.data[2] := $0100;
   MoveCursor.data[3] := $0380;
   MoveCursor.data[4] := $0540;
   MoveCursor.data[5] := $0100;
   MoveCursor.data[6] := $1110;
   MoveCursor.data[7] := $2108;
   MoveCursor.data[8] := $7FFC;
   MoveCursor.data[9] := $2108;
   MoveCursor.data[10] := $1110;
   MoveCursor.data[11] := $0100;
   MoveCursor.data[12] := $0540;
   MoveCursor.data[13] := $0380;
   MoveCursor.data[14] := $0100;
   MoveCursor.data[15] := $0000;
   MoveCursor.mask[0] := $0000;
   MoveCursor.mask[1] := $0000;
   MoveCursor.mask[2] := $0100;
   MoveCursor.mask[3] := $0380;
   MoveCursor.mask[4] := $0540;
   MoveCursor.mask[5] := $0100;
   MoveCursor.mask[6] := $1110;
   MoveCursor.mask[7] := $2108;
   MoveCursor.mask[8] := $7FFC;
   MoveCursor.mask[9] := $2108;
   MoveCursor.mask[10] := $1110;
   MoveCursor.mask[11] := $0100;
   MoveCursor.mask[12] := $0540;
   MoveCursor.mask[13] := $0380;
   MoveCursor.mask[14] := $0100;
   MoveCursor.mask[15] := $0000;
   MoveCursor.hotspot.v := 8;
   MoveCursor.hotspot.h := 7;
  end;
  procedure SizeCurs;
  begin
   SizeCursor.data[0] := $0000;
   SizeCursor.data[1] := $0000;
   SizeCursor.data[2] := $3800;
   SizeCursor.data[3] := $3000;
   SizeCursor.data[4] := $2800;
   SizeCursor.data[5] := $0400;
```

```
SizeCursor.data[6] := $0200;
SizeCursor.data[7] := $0100;
SizeCursor.data[8] := $0080;
SizeCursor.data[9] := $0040;
SizeCursor.data[10] := $0028;
SizeCursor.data[11] := $0018;
SizeCursor.data[12] := $0038;
SizeCursor.data[13] := $0000;
SizeCursor.data[14] := $0000;
SizeCursor.data[15] := $0000;

SizeCursor.mask[0] := $0000;
SizeCursor.mask[1] := $0000;
SizeCursor.mask[2] := $3800;
SizeCursor.mask[3] := $3000;
SizeCursor.mask[4] := $2800;
SizeCursor.mask[5] := $0400;
SizeCursor.mask[6] := $0200;
SizeCursor.mask[7] := $0100;
SizeCursor.mask[8] := $0080;
SizeCursor.mask[9] := $0040;
SizeCursor.mask[10] := $0028;
SizeCursor.mask[11] := $0018;
SizeCursor.mask[12] := $0038;
SizeCursor.mask[13] := $0000;
SizeCursor.mask[14] := $0000;
SizeCursor.mask[15] := $0000;
SizeCursor.hotspot.v := 2;
SizeCursor.hotspot.h := 2;
end;
procedure InitWindow;
begin
 HideAll;
 SetRect(TitleBar, Window.left - 1, Window.top - 19, Window.right, Window.top);
 SetRect(SizeBox, Window.right - 15, Window.bottom - 15, Window.right, Window.bottom);
 SetRect(EditArea, Window.left, Window.top, Window.right - 15, Window.bottom - 15);
 SetDrawingRect(Window);
 ShowDrawing;
end;
procedure Setup;
begin
 GetDrawingRect(Window);
 InitWindow;
 MoveCurs;
 SizeCurs;
 SquareCurs;
end;
procedure MoveWindow;
begin
 OffsetRect(Window, DeltaMouse.h, DeltaMouse.v);
 InitWindow;
end;
procedure SizeWindow;
```

```
begin
  Window.right := Window.right + DeltaMouse.h;
  Window.bottom := Window.bottom + DeltaMouse.v;
  InitWindow;
end;
procedure TrackMouse;
  var
    Event : EventRecord;
    MouseDown, MouseUp : Point;
begin
  repeat
    repeat
      GetMouse(MousePos.h, MousePos.v);
      MousePos.h := MousePos.h + Window.left;
      MousePos.v := MousePos.v + Window.top;
      if PtInRect(MousePos, TitleBar) then
        SetCursor(MoveCursor)
      else if PtInRect(MousePos, SizeBox) then
        SetCursor(SizeCursor)
      else if PtInRect(MousePos, EditArea) then
        SetCursor(SqCursor)
      else
        InitCursor;
    until GetNextEvent(MDownMask, Event);
    MouseDown := Event.where;
    repeat
    until GetNextEvent(MUpMask, Event);
    MouseUp := Event.where;
    DeltaMouse := MouseUp;
    SubPt(MouseDown, DeltaMouse);
    if PtInRect(MouseDown, TitleBar) then
      MoveWindow
    else if PtInRect(MouseDown, SizeBox) then
      SizeWindow;
  until MouseUp.v < 20;
  end;
begin
  Setup;
  TrackMouse;
end.
```

Examining the WindowManager Program

The WindowManager program allows the position of the window to be changed and the window to be resized. The routines that are demonstrated in the program on the drawing window are just as applicable to the text window. The program is divided into two main routines, the Setup procedure that performs the initialization required by the program and the TrackMouse procedure that performs the moving or resizing of the window.

As previously discussed, the SetUp procedure calls the InitWindow procedure to initialize the window. In addition, SetUp initializes MoveCursor, SizeCursor, and SquareCursor by the MoveCurs, SizeCurs, and SquareCurs procedures. These are standard cursor initialization procedures and are very similar to the ones discussed in Chapter 3.

After the program is initialized by the SetUp procedure, the TrackMouse procedure assumes control of the program. TrackMouse performs two distinct functions. First, it maintains the correct cursor in the appropriate area of the screen in much the same way as the IconEditor program. The only difference between the maintenance of the mouse in IconEditor and its maintenance in the WindowManager program is that the WindowManager program must track the mouse outside of the drawing window, whereas the entire screen of the IconEditor program is contained within the drawing area. This means that the results of the GetMouse call in the WindowManager program must be compensated by translating them from the local coordinate system into the global coordinate system. This is done by adding the left boundary of the window to the horizontal mouse position and the top boundary of the window to the vertical mouse position.

Alternatively, QuickDraw has a special procedure available that performs this same conversion. This procedure is called LocalToGlobal and is defined as

    procedure LocalToGlobal (var pt:Point);

LocalToGlobal converts the point defined by *pt* from the local coordinates of the grafPort associated with the window to a global coordinate system.

There is also a procedure, GlobalToLocal, that performs the opposite function of LocalToGlobal.

    procedure GlobalToLocal (var pt:Point);

The point defined by *pt* is converted from global coordinates to the local coordinate system as defined by the window's grafPort.

After the current mouse position has been adjusted to global coordinates, it is then used in the same way as demonstrated in the previous cursor demonstration program to maintain the cursor. This continues until a mouse button down event occurs, at which time the TrackMouse procedure performs its second function. The program records the position where the mouse button down event occurred by saving it in the MouseDown variable. It then waits until the mouse button is released. After the mouse button is released, it is possible to calculate the change in the mouse's position. It is this change in the mouse's position that, when applied correctly to the boundaries of the window, results in either the new position of the window or the new size of the window. The program calculates the variable DeltaMouse by using the SubPt procedure. SubPt is a QuickDraw procedure defined as

```
procedure SubPt (srcPt:Point; var dstPt:Point);
```

The SubPt procedure subtracts the point stored in srcPt from the point stored in *dstPt* and places the result in dstPt.

DeltaMouse now contains the mouse's change in position, which needs to be applied to the window. The MouseDown variable, in which the position of the mouse button down event is stored, can now be interrogated by the PtInRect procedure. If the mouse button down event occurred in the title bar, indicating that the window is moving, the MoveWindow procedure is called. If the mouse button down event occurred in the size box, the SizeWindow procedure is called. Each of these procedures applies DeltaMouse to the window and redisplays the window in its new size or position.

The MoveWindow procedure uses the OffsetRect procedure to apply the change in mouse position to the window. This changes the position of the window without changing its size. The InitWindow procedure is then called to redraw the window in its new position.

The SizeWindow procedure applies the change in mouse position in a different way. When the window is moved, as described above, it is only necessary to use the OffsetRect procedure to create the change. However, changing the size of the window does not change the location of the window, even though the bottom and right edges of the window move according to the change in the mouse's position. Adding the horizontal component of DeltaMouse to the right boundary of the window and the vertical component of DeltaMouse to the bottom boundary of the window causes the required changes in the window. As in MoveWindow, the InitWindow procedure is then called to redraw the window in its new size.

The program continues to repeat this loop, allowing the window to be moved and resized until the mouse is clicked within the menu bar. This action terminates the program.

Notice that the rectangle drawn in the window disappears if the window is sized down and then sized up again. Applications that use this resizing technique must redraw the window contents after resizing. The simplest way to redraw the window is to use the Quick-Draw picture facility when originally drawing the contents of the window. After the window has been sized, it is simple to redraw the contents without having to recall all the procedures originally involved in producing the window contents.

You may have noticed that the WindowManager program handles windows significantly slower than does the Macintosh itself when using windows in applications like MacWrite. The reason for this is that you are running a program (WindowManager) that is several steps removed from directly accessing the Toolbox procedures within the Macintosh. Because Macintosh Pascal is interpreted rather than compiled, each line of the program must be translated into actual machine language of 1's and 0's before it is executed. This translation is done while the program is running, which obviously requires a great deal of time. Of course, the closer you get to the Macintosh's Toolbox routines using compiled languages, the faster programs will operate.

Summary

This chapter examined the anatomy of the windows available through the Macintosh Pascal interpreter. It pointed out that, although the Macintosh Pascal interpreter does not allow any direct access to the Window Manager, it is still possible to create programs that exert a modicum of control over the window.

The two particular management features that were demonstrated in this chapter were the ability to move the drawing window or the text window about the screen and the ability to resize either of these windows using the mouse.

The effects of local and global coordinate systems were also discussed, along with techniques that permit conversion from one coordinate system to the other.

Finally, the chapter showed the problems inherent in the resizing of windows. It further indicated that, after resizing has been completed, it is necessary for an applications program to have the capability of redrawing the window.

6

Advanced Macintosh Programming

Until now the programs in this book have depended heavily on the libraries of Macintosh Pascal. A library is a collection of routines, functions, or procedures that can be accessed by a program. The routines contained in a library are there for a programmer's use and do not have to be declared or written by the programmer. This eliminates the need for the programmer to write routines to perform commonly used tasks in programs.

In this chapter we will explore ways in which we can access other controlling functions of the Macintosh Toolbox that are not implemented in Macintosh Pascal. This is principally achieved through the use of the InLine routine.

The InLine Routine

The Macintosh Pascal interpreter contains a special routine called InLine which, by disabling the parameter-checking procedures of Pascal, allows different parameter lists to be substituted wherever necessary. There are four variations of InLine that may be used. Which InLine variation you use depends upon which Toolbox procedure or function is to be called.

A Pascal function returns a value of one of three different sizes—a byte (eight bits), a word (sixteen bits), or a long word (thirty-two bits). The InLine functions do not care what the returned data type is. Their only concern is with the size of the result. This makes it possible to call all of the Toolbox functions using only three functions—BInLineF, WInLineF, and LInLineF. BInLineF is used for functions that yield a byte-size result. WInLineF is used for functions that yield a word-size result, and LInLineF is used to call functions that yield a long word-size result. InLineP is a fourth function used to call Toolbox procedures that do not return a value.

Though InLine might seem confusing upon first encounter, if you keep the following in mind you'll have no trouble putting InLine to work in your Pascal programs. BInLineF, WInLineF, and LInLineF are functions; that is, they return a single value as their result, just like any other Pascal function. InLineP is a procedure that, like other Pascal procedures, passes one or more values to the called procedure. These four InLine routines let you use any Toolbox procedure or function, whether they are directly available through Macintosh Pascal or not.

Unfortunately, the InLine routines have not been documented in any Apple publication. This makes their use rather difficult. However, this section of the book shows how accessing the four InLine routines is done and describes some of the functions and procedures that may be accessed by these routines.

WARNING: It is possible to destroy data or even the Macintosh Pascal disk itself by incorrect use of the InLine routines. Make sure you have a backup copy of your Pascal disk before attempting to use InLine in your own programs. Pay particular attention to functions that concern folders, files, and disk access. These functions have the potential to erase things you may not want to erase. Whenever a dangerous situation presents itself in the following discussion, you will be informed about the harm that may result from misuse of the InLine routines.

The Inline routines work by referencing a *trap number.* A trap number is the number associated with each procedure or function in the Macintosh Toolbox. In other words, instead of using the function or procedure name to call the Toolbox function or procedure, you should give the appropriate InLine routine the trap number of the function or procedure you want to use. Appendix C gives a complete list of Toolbox procedures and functions together with their associated trap numbers.

In the InLine routine, the first parameter in the parameter list is the trap number of the procedure or function that you want to call. Any successive parameters given to InLine are those required by the procedure or function being called.

The following listing uses the FrameRect procedure to demonstrate the use of the InLine procedure called InLineP.

```
program InLineDemo;
  const
    SetRect = $A8A7;
    FrameRect = $A8A1;
  type
    rect = array[1..4] of integer;
  var
    Square : Rect;
begin
  Hideall;
  ShowDrawing;
  InLineP(SetRect, @Square, 100, 100, 200, 200);
  InLineP(FrameRect, Square);
end.
```

In this program, the procedures SetRect and FrameRect are called indirectly through the InLineP procedure. The first parameter is a constant that has been set to the trap number of the appropriate procedure. Simply select the proper trap number and give it to the InLine routine, followed by the necessary parameters of the function or procedure you wish to use. In this fashion, InLine gives you access to most of the useful Toolbox utilities.

You may also have noticed that the data type Rect has been explicitly defined as an array of four integers. This has been done to demonstrate an alternative to predefined data types, functions, and procedures. When a program references a library function or data type, Macintosh Pascal includes in your program the entire library containing the definition for the referenced item, regardless of whether references are made to anything else in the library. In this program, for instance, the Rect data type would only have been referenced to a QuickDraw library entry. If Rect had not been explicitly defined, Macintosh Pascal would have defaulted to including the QuickDraw library references into your program. These libraries can take up as much as 4K bytes of memory that otherwise could be used for your program.

Although sidestepping library references gains application space, it involves some disadvantages. First, you always have to define explicitly the data types required by your program. Aside from being tedious, this is also poor programming practice. If, for example, Apple decides to change one of the data types, you will have to go through every program that uses this data type and change its definition to match the new definition. By using the library references, you would only have to get an updated Macintosh Pascal disk containing all of the changes within its libraries.

Another problem, illustrated in the above program, is that although this explicit definition of Rect is suitable in that it provides enough space to store the definition of a rectangle, it does not work if it becomes necessary to refer to the record fields of right, top, left, and bottom. This limits the use and application of the explicit data type definition.

One last point on using InLine. Notice the use of the "at" symbol (@) preceding the variable Square. As you may know, this symbol is an operator that returns the memory address of the variable it precedes. When the address of a parameter is passed to the function or procedure, it is called *call-by-reference*. In Pascal, the default parameter passing mechanism, in which the value of a parameter is passed and not its address, is *call-by-value*. You may override this default mechanism by preceding the formal parameter with the Pascal keyword **var** when the function or procedure is defined.

For example, the procedure SetRect is defined as

procedure SetRect (var r:Rect; left, top, right, bottom:integer);

In this case, the procedure explicitly requests the address of rectangle r. The remaining four parameters are integers and merely have their values passed normally. Always use the "@" operator whenever the procedure or function defines the parameter with the **var** keyword.

Whenever you access a function or procedure through an InLine routine, you must be especially careful to supply the proper parameters. InLine does not check your parameter list for the proper format. If any of the parameters do not match, or if there are too few or too many parameters, the results are unpredictable and potentially disastrous.

The Menu Manager

The Menu Manager consists of a set of routines in the Toolbox that support the use of menus by an application. Menu control is a very important function for the Macintosh.

With menus, the user of an application may browse through the choices that are available without necessarily choosing any of them. Menus eliminate the need for a user to remember special commands or keystrokes. A user may open any menu at any time by moving the cursor up to the menu bar and pressing the mouse button over one of the displayed menu titles. This highlights the menu title, and the corresponding menu drops down. By moving the mouse down while holding the mouse button down, each item in the menu is highlighted. If the mouse button is released over one of these menu items, the item blinks to indicate that it has been selected. The menu then disappears. The menu title remains highlighted, however, until the application has completed the action associated with the selected item.

The menu bar always appears at the top of the Macintosh's screen. It is 20 pixels high and appears in front of everything else on the screen except the cursor. It is a white bar with a thin black lower edge. As shown in Figure 6-1, menu titles appear in the menu bar in the system font of Chicago in 12-point size.

The first menu title that normally appears in an application is the

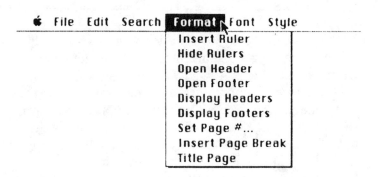

Figure 6-1. *Sample menu bar from MacWrite*

Apple menu. This menu contains selections that access the desk accessories. Some applications may not support the use of desk accessories, so the Apple may not always be present.

Menus sometimes have all of their items disabled (as in MacWrite when there is no open file). The Menu Manager causes menu titles to appear dimmed or unhighlighted, thus preventing their selection with the mouse.

The menu bar may contain up to 16 menu titles. Depending upon the length of the menu titles, however, it is usually not possible or even necessary to use all 16 titles.

A menu consists of a number of lines of text that, like the titles, always appear in the 12-point system font. The items appear in a shadowed rectangle that, when activated, always appears in front of everything else on the screen except the cursor. Each line of text may take a number of variations:

- An icon may appear to the left of the item text.

- A check mark may appear to the left of the item text and/or an icon.

- The COMMAND key symbol and a character may appear to the right of the item text. This indicates that the particular menu item may be invoked from the keyboard by pressing the COMMAND key and the specified character key.

- The item may appear in a character style other than the standard, such as bold, shadow, underline, italic, outline, or any combination of these.

- The item may appear dimmed, indicating that the item is disabled and may not be selected.

- The menu may contain up to twenty entries, some of which may be blank items or lines of dashes used to separate groups of items.

Creating Menus

Macintosh applications have several ways to define menus and even alter their appearance. Menus may also be stored in an area of memory known as a *resource file*. It is, however, outside the scope of this book and beyond Macintosh Pascal's ability to develop full-scale applications.

Two routines may be used to create menus from an applications program—NewMenu and AppendMenu. NewMenu initializes space in memory for the menu and returns a *handle* to this data space. Essentially, a handle is a pointer to a pointer. This process is called *double indirection*, and it is used for efficient memory management. It is not necessary to know the exact format of the menu data structure because all interaction is done through the Menu Manager routines stored in the Toolbox. The NewMenu function is defined as follows:

```
function NewMenu (menuID:integer; menuTitle:Str255):MenuHandle;
```

NewMenu returns a handle (of type MenuHandle) that is used to refer to the menu you wish to create. Essentially, the NewMenu function is used to inform the Menu Manager that you will need space in memory for a new menu that will have the ID *menuID* and the title *menuTitle*. The new menu is created empty, so it is necessary to use the routine AppendMenu to fill it with the items you want. The menu ID should be a positive integer greater than zero.

The AppendMenu routine is used to set up the items in the menu and is defined as

```
procedure AppendMenu (theMenu:MenuHandle; data:Str255);
```

AppendMenu adds an item or items in data to the end of the menu specified by *theMenu*. The data string may be blank but it should not be null. This string contains the text of the item or items you want to append to the menu. Table 6-1 shows some special *metacharacters* that have special significance for the Menu Manager.

Here are some examples of the AppendMenu routine as it may be used:

1. AppendMenu (MyMenu,"Item 1;Item 2");

2. AppendMenu (MyMenu,"Item 1;(;Item 2");

3. AppendMenu (MyMenu,"Item 1/1;Item 2/2");

4. AppendMenu (MyMenu,"Item 1<S;Item 2<B");

Example 1 sets up a menu with two items in it. The items appear in plain text, with no keyboard equivalent, one beneath the other. Example 2 sets up a menu with three items, one of which is blank and disabled. Example 3 sets up a menu with two items in it, each with a keyboard equivalent. Example 4 sets up a menu with two items in it. The first item is drawn in the shadow character style, and the second is drawn in the bold style.

After the menus have been initialized by NewMenu and sent to the Menu Manager via the AppendMenu command, the menu bar must be formed and drawn. Several procedures and functions are

Table 6-1. *MetaCharacters*

MetaCharacter	Meaning
; or Return	Separates multiple items.
^	Followed by an icon number, adds that icon to the item.
!	Followed by a character marks that item with that character.
<	Followed by B, I, U, O, or S, sets the character style of the item.
/	Followed by a character, associates a keyboard equivalent with that item.
(	Disables the item.

available to help do this. The first thing that must be done is to create a list of the menus that will make up the menu bar. This is done by using the InsertMenu procedure. The InsertMenu procedure is defined as

procedure InsertMenu (theMenu:MenuHandle; beforeID:integer);

The InsertMenu procedure forms the menu list by inserting the handle of the menu referenced by the variable *theMenu* before the menu whose menu ID is referenced by the variable *beforeID*. If beforeID is set to 0, the new menu will be added after the last menu in the list.

When the menu list has been created through the use of the InsertMenu procedure, the menu bar must be displayed. This is done by the DrawMenuBar procedure, which is defined as

procedure DrawMenuBar;

DrawMenuBar redraws the menu bar, incorporating any changes that have been made since the last time the menu bar was drawn. This procedure should always be called after invoking any procedure that makes any changes to the menu list. The new menu list will not become active until this procedure is called; nor will the user be aware that there may be a new menu present.

In summary, the following steps must be taken to create a set of Macintosh menus:

1. Initialize the menu by calling the NewMenu function.

2. Set up the menu using the AppendMenu procedure.

3. After the menus are set up, use the InsertMenu procedure to create the menu list.

4. After the menu list has been created, call the DrawMenuBar procedure to actually draw the new menu bar and activate the menus.

Closing Menus

Often during the course of an applications program, some menus will no longer be required or new menus may be needed. Certain procedures allow a programmer to change the contents of the menu list while an applications program is executing.

The DeleteMenu procedure may be used to remove a menu from the menu list. DeleteMenu is defined as

```
procedure DeleteMenu (menuID:integer);
```

The menu identified by *menuID* will be deleted from the menu list. If there is no menu with the specified ID, the procedure will have no effect.

To completely clear the menu list, the ClearMenuBar procedure may be used:

```
procedure ClearMenuBar;
```

ClearMenuBar deletes all the menus in the current menu bar, allowing the programmer to start afresh and create a completely new menu list.

It is possible that a program will need two sets of menus, each menu list being used for different reasons. Two Menu Manager routines let two menus exist without regenerating the menu specifications each time a new menu is required. The first method involves using a function that creates a copy of the current menu list and returns a handle to it. The GetMenuBar function is defined as

```
function GetMenuBar:Handle;
```

After this procedure has been called, the menu list may be modified using any of the routines already discussed that affect the menu list. The old menu list may be reused at a later time by using the SetMenuBar procedure, which is defined as

```
procedure SetMenuBar (menuList:Handle);
```

The SetMenuBar procedure will reinstate the menu list indicated by the handle *menuList* as the current menu list.

These two procedures are important to programs that run under the Macintosh Pascal interpreter and need to take advantage of the Menu Manager routines to control program flow. The Macintosh Pascal interpreter is already using the menu bar to control its own program flow; therefore, these menus must be saved at the beginning of a program, using the GetMenuBar function, and restored at the termination of the program, using the SetMenuBar procedure.

Remember to use the DrawMenuBar procedure after each change to the menu list, or else the new menu list will not become active. This is especially important when you are running a program under the Macintosh Pascal interpreter. If the menu bar is not restored and activated, you will lose control of the interpreter and will not be able to quit Macintosh Pascal.

Using Menus in Applications

Now that the procedures for creating and displaying the menu bar have been introduced, it is necessary for an applications program to know when an item from a menu is selected, so that it can act upon that selection. In addition, an applications program must also recognize and act upon a press of the COMMAND key in conjunction with a character key if some menu items have been set up with COMMAND key equivalents. Two routines perform this function, the MenuSelect function and the MenuKey function.

When a mouse button down event occurs in the menu bar, an applications program should call the MenuSelect function to determine the result of the mouse action. The MenuSelect function then takes over the tracking of the mouse and returns any results. The MenuSelect function is defined as

function MenuSelect (startPt:Point):longint;

The *startPt* variable should be set to the point at which the mouse button down event occurred (the where field from the event record). Once the MenuSelect function has been called, it tracks the mouse, pulls down menus as required, and highlights the menu items as the mouse moves over them. When the mouse button is finally released, the MenuSelect function returns two integers. The first integer is in the high-word portion of the longint result. The second integer is in the low-word portion of the longint result. The high-word portion contains the menu ID of the menu in which the final selection occurs. The low-word portion contains the item number of the final selection. As in Figure 6-2, items are numbered from the top of the menu to the bottom, starting with the value 1.

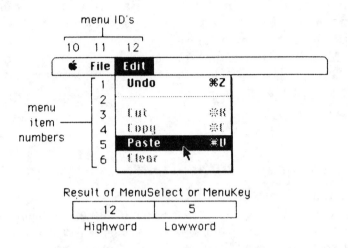

Figure 6-2. *Menu selections*

After a selection has been made, the MenuSelect function blinks the item selected, releases the menu, and highlights the menu title. Blinking is most easily controlled with the Control Panel desk accessory. After the menu item selection, control is passed back to the applications program to process the selection. Once the applications program has processed the selection, it should call the HiliteMenu procedure with menuID set to 0 to clear the highlighting of the menu title, thus completing the processing of a selection.

If no selection is made, either by the mouse being released over a disabled item or by its being outside the menu itself, MenuSelect returns 0.

Both the MenuKey function and the MenuSelect function return the same types of results. The difference between the two is that MenuKey determines whether a keystroke invoked a menu item. MenuKey is defined as

function MenuKey (ch:char):longint;

The MenuKey function should be called when a key down event occurs with the COMMAND key held down. The character typed should be passed to the MenuKey function in the *ch* field of the parameter list. The MenuKey function then returns the same result as if the item had been selected from the menu itself, and will, in the same way as MenuSelect, highlight the menu title of the menu. Once again, after processing the result of MenuKey, it is necessary to call HiliteMenu(0) to remove the menu title's highlighting. If no item in any menu with the COMMAND key equivalent exists, MenuKey returns 0.

In the earlier discussion of the MenuSelect and MenuKey functions, mention was made of the HiliteMenu procedure. The HiliteMenu is the procedure you use after processing a menu selection when processing is completed. The HiliteMenu procedure may be used to highlight any menu title and is defined as

```
procedure HiliteMenu (menuID:integer);
```

HiliteMenu highlights the menu title specified by *menuID*. If the title is already highlighted, calling this procedure has no effect. If the menuID is set to 0 or is set to a menuID that does not exist in the menu list, then any menu that is highlighted is unhighlighted. This procedure should be called to reverse the effects of MenuSelect or MenuKey when an applications program has completed processing a menu selection.

When an applications program is running, some menu functions may not be applicable to whatever is being performed at that time. For example, in the MacWrite word processing program, the Cut item in the Edit menu is not available until the text to be cut has been selected. The Menu Manager supplies two routines that are used to enable or disable (signified by dimming the item) a menu item, either preventing a menu item from being selected or allowing it to be selected.

The routine that disables a menu item is the DisableItem procedure. It is defined as

```
procedure DisableItem (theMenu:MenuHandle; item:integer);
```

DisableItem disables the menu item specified by *item* in the menu pointed to by *theMenu*. If item is set to 0, the entire menu is disabled. If the entire menu is disabled, the menu title is dimmed, but it is necessary to call DrawMenuBar to display the dimmed menu title.

EnableItem performs the opposite function to DisableItem. It is defined as

```
procedure EnableItem (theMenu:MenuHandle; item:integer);
```

EnableItem enables the item number specified by *item* in the menu pointed to by *theMenu*. If item is set to 0, the entire menu is enabled. However, it is necessary to call DrawMenuBar to display the new appearance of the menu title.

Sometimes an application contains menu items that have a permanent effect on a program's processing after the item has been selected. An example of this is the Grid item in the Goodies menu of MacPaint. After Grid has been selected, the cursor moves only to the points of an invisible grid mapped onto the drawing window. Lines or shapes are drawn on these invisible grid lines. A check appears next to the Grid item in the Goodies menu to signify that the grid is in effect. Selecting the Grid item again turns off the grid feature, and the check mark disappears. The check mark is a Macintosh User Interface requirement that informs the person using a program about the menu items in effect at any one time.

The procedure that allows menu items to be checked in this way is the CheckItem procedure:

```
procedure CheckItem (theMenu:MenuHandle; item:integer;
    checked:boolean);
```

When CheckItem is called, with checked equal to the Boolean value of True, a check mark appears beside the specified item in the menu pointed to by *theMenu*. To reverse the effect (to remove the check mark from an item), call the procedure with checked equal to the Boolean value of False. Before calling this procedure, you must always have the item set to item number and theMenu set to the MenuHandle of the menu in which the item resides.

Two final Menu Manager routines may be useful to the Macintosh Pascal programmer. These two routines allow an applications program to determine and set a menu item's appearance in any desired character style. The two procedures are SetItemStyle and GetItemStyle and are defined as

```
procedure SetItemStyle (theMenu:MenuHandle; item:integer;
    chStyle:style);

procedure GetItemStyle (theMenu:MenuHandle; item:integer; var
    chStyle:style);
```

SetItemStyle is used to change the character style of a menu item's appearance, and GetItemStyle is used to find a menu item's appearance. SetItemStyle (MyMenu,2,[bold,Underline]) sets the second item in MyMenu to boldfacing underlined character style. GetItemStyle returns the current style settings of the menu item in variable *chStyle*.

This completes the review of the Menu Manager routines that may be usefully and safely called from a Macintosh Pascal program, using the four InLine routines supplied by Macintosh Pascal. An excellent example of their use may be found in the TextEditor program that accompanies the Macintosh Pascal disk. This program should be studied before you attempt to use these routines in one of your own applications programs.

The Window Manager

An earlier section of this book described a program that provided some primitive Window Manager functions available from Macintosh Pascal's own libraries. This section describes the set of routines stored in the Toolbox; they make up the Window Manager.

The Window Manager can display several different types of windows. An applications program can display a predefined type of window known as a *document window*. A document window contains a title bar, size box, and scroll bars. Other types of windows, such as dialog windows, may be created when you use other parts of the Toolbox. Windows created by an application are known as *application windows*, whereas windows created by the system, such as desk accessory windows, are known as *system windows*.

An applications program may create and control as many windows as necessary, depending on the limitations of available memory. Several different windows may exist on the desktop simultaneously. The Window Manager keeps track of the different windows on the desktop as the user moves them from one place to another, resizes them, or activates them one at a time.

Regardless of how many windows are on the desktop at any one time, there is always only one active window. The active window is the one into which a user may enter or edit information. This window has its title bar highlighted to distinguish it from other windows on the desktop, and it is always the front-most window on the desktop. The Window Manager keeps track of which portions of the various windows are visible and which portions of the windows need to be redrawn due to movement of the windows by the user.

The Window Manager also contains a set of routines that allows a standard set of mouse actions to have a similar effect inside each of the various windows that may appear on the desktop. These actions are

1. Clicking in an inactive window makes it the active window and brings it to the foreground with a highlighted title bar.

2. Clicking inside the close box of a window removes the window from the desktop.

3. Dragging while inside the title bar (except in the close box) moves the window around the screen.

4. Dragging inside the size box resizes the window.

A window is made up of two distinct regions: The *content region*, which is the area in which the applications program draws, and the *structure region*, which is the entire window. The structure region contains the content region plus the window frame. When a window is created, the content region is defined by a rectangle lying within the portRect rectangle of the grafPort that will be set to the window. This rectangle defines the area in which the applications program will draw the window.

Windows are drawn on the screen in a special grafPort that has the entire screen as its portRect. This grafPort is known as the *Window Manager Port*. All windows drawn by the Window Manager are drawn in the Window Manager Port. In turn, each window has its own grafPort set up by the applications program for drawing.

The Window Manager maintains one other important region, called the *update region*. Areas of the content region that need to be redrawn are accumulated by the Window Manager into the update region. The applications program is responsible for redrawing the contents of the update region after an *update event* has occurred. An update event is a special event (such as resizing or activation) that is posted to the event queue by the Window Manager each time the contents of a window need to be redrawn.

Drawing a window is a two-step process. When the command to draw the window is issued, the Window Manager draws the window on the screen. The manager then posts an update event into the event queue, and the application draws the contents of the window.

Periodically, the application should check the event queue for update events with the GetNextEvent function using the UpdateMask and ActiveMask constants. If one is found, the window should be redrawn.

Only Window Manager routines applicable to Macintosh Pascal programs are discussed in the following text. Some of the other available Window Manager routines can only be used by a true Macintosh application. Some Window Manager functions are used by Macintosh Pascal itself, and calling these routines could interfere with the operation of the interpreter.

Inside the Window Manager

The Window Manager maintains a record data structure known as a *window record* for each window created by an applications program. It is not important for the programmer to know the exact structure of the window record. Knowing its size, however, is important because the storage area for this record must exist in the applications program. The window record requires 156 bytes of storage and may be declared as follows:

```
type
   WindowRecord:packed array [1..78] of integer;
var
   WindowStorage:WindowRecord;
```

Once again we have merely allocated the appropriate amount of memory for a window record. We have not defined the exact structure and will not do so for the purposes of this discussion.

A pointer to the WindowRecord is also required. This may be declared as

```
type
   WindowPtr:^WindowRecord;
var
   theWindow:WindowPtr;
```

Declarations of this type are required for each window displayed by an applications program.

The NewWindow function is the routine used to create a new window. It is defined as follows:

```
function NewWindow (wStorage:Ptr; boundsRect:Rect; title:Str255;
    visible:boolean; procID:integer; behind:WindowPtr;
    goAwayFlag:boolean; refCon:longint):WindowPtr;
```

The NewWindow function creates a new window, as specified by its parameter list, and returns a handle to it. The variable *wStorage* is a pointer to the storage area for the window record. In the examples of the declaration above, the wStorage parameter would be the pointer theWindow. The *boundsRect* parameter determines the initial size and location of the window in a manner similar to that done for the Macintosh Pascal drawing window through the SetDrawingRect procedure. The *title* parameter refers to the window's title, which will appear centered in the window's title bar.

If the visible parameter is set to True, the Window Manager will draw the window immediately. How the Window Manager draws the new window depends upon the *behind* parameter.

The behind parameter determines whether or not the window is in front of any other windows currently on the screen. If the behind field is set to Nil, the new window is drawn behind all the other windows. If the behind field is set to the pointer of another window, the new window is drawn behind the window indicated. Placing the window in front of all the other windows on the screen is done by setting behind to −1. When placed in the front-most position, the Window Manager deactivates the previously active window and creates an activate event for the new window. In addition, if the *goAwayFlag* parameter is set to True, the Window Manager draws a close box in the title bar of the new window.

The *procID* parameter determines what kind of window will be drawn by the Window Manager. Any one of the following constants may be used:

Constant	Description
0	Standard document window
1	Alert box or dialog box
2	Same as alert box but no shadow
3	Modeless dialog box
16	Desk Accessory window

The *refCon* parameter is set and used only by the application and has no effect on the Window Manager. This variable may be used for storing a handle to the contents of a window.

After an application has finished with a window, it can use the CloseWindow procedure to remove the window from the screen.

procedure CloseWindow (theWindow:WindowPtr);

The CloseWindow procedure removes the window indicated by *theWindow* from the screen. Any update events that may be pending for this window are discarded when this procedure is called. This procedure may also create an activate event for another window if the window being closed is the front-most window.

Window Titles

Two routines may be used to interrogate and set the title of a window. These are useful for applications that need to change the title of the window. For example, when creating a new file in MacWrite, the name of the default document window is Untitled. However, when the contents of the window have been saved as a file, the window title becomes the name of the file. The first of the routines to name a window title is GetWTitle, which is defined as

procedure GetWTitle (theWindow:WindowPtr; var title:Str255);

GetWTitle returns the title of the window indicated by *theWindow* in the *title* variable.
SetWTitle is used to change the window title. It is defined as

procedure SetWTitle (theWindow:WindowPtr; title:Str255);

SetWTitle changes the title of the window designated by *theWindow* to the title specified by *title*. SetWTitle performs any necessary redrawing of the window to fit the new title into the title bar.

Window Manipulation

All window manipulation is initiated by the user of a program when he or she moves, clicks, or drags the mouse in the different regions of windows displayed on the screen at any one time. Although it is the responsibility of the applications program to call the routines necessary to satisfy a user's needs, the program must first determine where the mouse button down event occurred in order to determine the appropriate routine to call. This is done by using the FindWindow function, which is defined as

```
function FindWindow (thePt:Point; var
    whichWindow:WindowPtr):integer;
```

Following the occurrence of a mouse button down event, the application should call FindWindow with *thePt* set to the point where the mouse button down event occurred. This should be in global coordinates obtained from the where field in the event record. To indicate where the mouse button down event occurred, the FindWindow function returns one of the following predefined constants. (Note that Apple's technical documentation refers to the title bar as a "drag region," the size box as a "grow region," and the close box as a "go away region.")

Constant	Value	Description
inDesk	0	In none of the following regions
inMenuBar	1	In the MenuBar
inSysWindow	2	In a system window
inContent	3	In the content region (except the grow region if it is active)
inDrag	4	In the drag region
inGrow	5	In the grow region (active window only)
inGoAway	6	In the go away region (active window only)

If the mouse button down event occurs in a window displayed on the screen, the *whichWindow* field will have a pointer indicating the window in which the mouse button down took place.

The program can take appropriate action after it has used the FindWindow procedure to determine which window had the mouse button down event. There are a number of procedures available to the WindowManager program for determining this.

If the mouse button down event occurred in the close box of an active window, the required action is the removal of the window from the screen. This is done by using the TrackGoAway function and the HideWindow procedure. TrackGoAway is defined as

```
function TrackGoAway (theWindow:WindowPtr; thePt:Point):boolean;
```

The TrackGoAway function should be called after a mouse button down event has occurred in the close box. The *thePt* parameter should be set to the position at which the mouse button down event occurred. This is in global coordinates and is easily obtained from the "where" field in the event record. The *theWindow* parameter should be set to the window pointer obtained from the FindWindow procedure. TrackGoAway tracks the position of the mouse until a mouse button up event occurs. During the tracking, and while the mouse remains in the close box, the TrackGoAway function causes the close box to be highlighted. If the mouse moves outside the close box, the highlighting is removed. After a mouse button up event occurs, TrackGoAway returns control to the calling program, yielding True if the mouse button up event occurred in the close box. If the mouse button up event did not occur in the close box, False is returned.

A TrackGoAway result of True indicates to the applications program that the window should be removed from the screen. This is done by the HideWindow procedure.

procedure HideWindow (theWindow:WindowPtr);

HideWindow removes the window pointed to by *theWindow*. This procedure should only be called for an active window, as it removes the active window, brings the window behind the removed window to the front, highlights that window, and creates the appropriate activate events.

The opposite of the HideWindow procedure is the ShowWindow procedure, defined as

procedure ShowWindow (theWindow:WindowPtr);

The ShowWindow procedure makes the window indicated by the-Window field visible on the screen. The window displayed on the screen is never the front-most window.

The ShowWindow procedure is not usually called as a result of a mouse button down event. Instead, it is more likely to be called as a result of a user-selected item from a menu.

If the FindWindow procedure has indicated that a mouse button down event occurred in a window other than the active window, the window in which the mouse button down event occurred becomes the active window. Two procedures are required to activate the window. The first of these procedures is the BringToFront procedure, defined as

procedure BringToFront (theWindow:WindowPtr);

The BringToFront procedure brings the window indicated by *theWindow* to the front of all the other windows on the screen and redraws the window.

After the BringToFront procedure has been used to bring the window to the front, use the HiLiteWindow procedure to make it the active window. This procedure is defined as

procedure HiLiteWindow (theWindow:WindowPtr; fHilite:boolean);

If *fHilite* equals True, the HiLiteWindow procedure highlights the window pointed to by *theWindow*. If fHilite equals False, then the HiLiteWindow performs the opposite action by unhighlighting the window. This action can be demonstrated by setting the Macintosh Pascal edit window to cover one-half of the screen and the Drawing window to cover the other half. By moving the mouse back and forth between the windows and clicking in alternate windows, you will see the title bar highlight change from window to window.

An alternative procedure, SelectWindow, performs the actions of both BringToFront and HiLiteWindow, essentially making any window active through one procedure call. The SelectWindow procedure is defined as

procedure SelectWindow (theWindow:WindowPtr);

The SelectWindow procedure makes the window pointed to by *theWindow* the active window by deactivating the currently active window, bringing the selected window to the front and activating it.

The active window may always be determined by using the FrontWindow function, as shown:

function FrontWindow:WindowPtr;

This function simply returns a pointer to the currently active window.

Determination by the FindWindow procedure that a mouse button down event has occurred in the title bar of a window informs an applications program that the user of the program wishes to move the position of that particular window to a new position on the screen. This movement is done by the DragWindow procedure, defined as

```
procedure DragWindow (theWindow:WindowPtr; startPt:Point;
    boundsRect:Rect);
```

The DragWindow procedure is called after a mouse button down event has occurred in the title bar of the window pointed to by *the Window*. The *startPt* parameter is set to the position at which the mouse button was pressed. This position should be in global coordinates; it is obtained from the where field in the event record. DragWindow tracks the mouse until a mouse button up event occurs. As it is tracking, DragWindow pulls a gray outline of the window around the screen, following the path of the mouse. After the mouse button up event occurs, DragWindow redraws the window and makes it the active window. The *boundsRect* parameter is used to limit the movement of the window. The DragWindow procedure will not redraw the window if the mouse moves outside of the rectangle specified by boundsRect. The value of (4, 24, 508, 338) is most often used as a boundary for boundsRect. Using this value ensures that at least four pixels of the title bar are always visible on the screen.

An indication by the FindWindow procedure that a mouse button down event has occurred in the size box of a window informs an applications program that the user wishes to resize the window, making it larger or smaller. A mouse button down event in a size box can only occur in the active window. After the event has occurred, the applications program should call the GrowWindow function, which performs the resizing of the window. The GrowWindow function is defined as

```
function GrowWindow (theWindow:WindowPtr; startPt:Point;
    sizeRect:Rect):longint;
```

The GrowWindow function should be called after a mouse button down event has occurred in the size box of the active window pointed to by *theWindow*. The field *startPt* should be set to the position where the mouse button down event occurred in global coordinates. The GrowWindow function, performing in much the same way as the DragWindow procedure, tracks the mouse around the screen until a mouse button up event is recorded. As the mouse moves about the screen, GrowWindow pulls a variable-sized image of the window around the screen in response to the movements of the mouse. This image is similar to the outlined window seen when dragging a window by its title bar. GrowWindow creates a gray outline of the title bar, scroll bar, and size box, but the window is anchored in its upper left corner. When the mouse button up event occurs, GrowWindow redraws the window in its new size. It does not redraw the contents of a newly exposed content region. This must be done by the applications program.

The *sizeRect* parameter functions in a manner similar to the boundsRect parameter in DragWindow. It specifies the minimum and maximum sizes of a window. These minimum and maximum sizes represent the rectangle structure as follows:

```
sizeRect.top     = minimum vertical measurement
sizeRect.left    = minimum horizontal measurement
sizeRect.bottom  = maximum vertical measurement
sizeRect.right   = maximum horizontal measurement
```

After the GrowWindow function is complete, the actual size of the window is returned in the longint result. The high-order word contains the vertical measurement in pixels, while the low-order word contains the horizontal measurement in pixels. GrowWindow returns a value of 0 if the size of the window does not change.

After the GrowWindow function returns control to the calling program, it is necessary to reset the grafPort of the newly sized window to its new dimensions. This is done by passing the result of the GrowWindow function to the SizeWindow procedure. The Size-Window procedure is defined as

```
procedure SizeWindow (theWindow:windowPtr; w, h:integer;
   fUpdate:boolean);
```

The SizeWindow procedure resets the size of the window's graf-Port to the new size of the window. This procedure should always be called after the GrowWindow function. The parameter *theWindow* should be set to point to the window that has just been resized. The *w* parameter should contain the low-order word of the result of GrowWindow, and *h* should be set to the high-order word of the GrowWindow result. If *fUpdate* is set to True, SizeWindow will accumulate the newly exposed area of the content region into the update region. However, if fUpdate is False, the applications program must redraw the newly exposed content region itself.

You may have noticed that the w and h parameters are integers contained within the long integer result from GrowWindow. You should use the two ToolBox utilities HiWord and LoWord to assist you in your conversion of the long integer value into the two integer parameters.

```
function HiWord (x:longint):integer;
function LoWord (x:longint):integer;
```

Function HiWord returns the high-order word of the parameter x. Conversely, LoWord returns the low-order word of x. Most applications programs would contain the following program segment:

```
result := GrowWindow(currentWindow, startWindowPt, sizeLimits);
    if result <> 0 then
    SizeWindow (currentWindow, HiWord(result), LoWord(result), True);
```

In this example, the result is a long integer that must be split into two discrete integers if SizeWindow is to perform its function properly. The parameter *currentWindow* points to the currently active window. *StartWindowPt* is the point at which the mouse button down event occurred, thereby initiating the resizing of the window. The maximum and minimum sizes of the window are specified by *sizeLimits*. If a resizing is to take place (because *result* is not equal to 0), the SizeWindow procedure is called, using the functions HiWord and LoWord to break the long integer result into the two required integers. For simplicity in this case, a constant value of True is used for fUpdate.

The Manager Program

For those of you interested in writing a program that controls menus or windows, here is a sample program that does both. As you type the program into Macintosh Pascal, examine each line to understand its purpose. If you decide not to dissect each program line while typing, then read through this chapter again to find out why each program line is in the program and what it does. Remember to save your typing frequently using the Save option of the File menu.

```
program Manager;
  const
{**** Menu Manager Trap Numbers ****}
   InitMenus = $A930;
   NewMenu = $A931;
   DisposeMenu = $A932;
   AppendMenu = $A933;
   ClearMenuBar = $A934;
   InsertMenu = $A935;
   DeleteMenu = $A936;
   DrawMenuBar = $A937;
   HiliteMenu = $A938;
   EnableItem = $A939;
   DisableItem = $A93A;
   GetMenuBar = $A93B;
   SetMenuBar = $A93C;
   MenuSelect = $A93D;
   MenuKey = $A93E;
   AddResMenu = $A94D;

{**** Event Manager Trap Numbers ****}
   GetNextEvent = $A970;

{**** Toolbox Utility Trap Numbers ****}
   HiWord = $A86A;
   Loword = $A86B;

{**** Window Manager Trap Numbers ****}
   CloseWindow = $A92D;
   GetNewWindow = $A9BD;
   NewWindow = $A913;
   FindWindow = $A92C;
   DragWindow = $A925;

{**** QuickDraw Trap Numbers ****}
   SetPort = $A873;

{**** Program Constants ****}
   EventMask = 14; {*** mouse button down, up, and key down events***}
   MouseDown = 1;
   MouseUp = 2;
   MouseUpMask = 4;
   KeyDown = 3;
   InMenuBar = 1;
   InDrag = 4;
   ItemMenu = 100;
   ObjectMenu = 101;

  type
   Handle = ^Longint;
{**** Working Storage for Window Manager ****}
   WindowRecord = array[1..98] of char;
   WindowPtr = ^WindowRecord;
```

```pascal
var
  OldMenuBar : Handle;
  Menu : array[1..2] of Handle;
  MenuTitle : string[10];
  Done, Temp : boolean;
  Event : EventRecord;
  WindowStorage : WindowRecord;
  DispWindow, whichWindow, TheWindow : Longint;
  DragRect, Window, Paper : Rect;

procedure InitWindow;
begin
{**** Get Window from resource file, Set size, and display it ****}
  DispWindow := LInLineF(GetNewWindow, 256, @WindowStorage, pointer(-1));
  SetRect(Window, 5, 50, 300, 200);
  DispWindow := LInLineF(NewWindow, @WindowStorage, Window, 'Menu Demo', true, 4,
       pointer(-1), false, nil);
  InLineP(SetPort, DispWindow);
end;

procedure SetUp;
begin
  HideAll;
  InitWindow;
{**** Save Macintosh Pascal's Menus ***}
  OldMenuBar := Pointer(LInLineF(GetMenuBar));
  InLineP(ClearMenuBar);
{**** Set up and display our menus ****}
  MenuTitle := 'Items';
  Menu[1] := Pointer(LInLineF(NewMenu, ItemMenu, MenuTitle));
  MenuTitle := 'Objects';
  Menu[2] := Pointer(LInLineF(NewMenu, ObjectMenu, MenuTitle));
  InLineP(AppendMenu, Menu[1], 'Item 1/1;Item 2/2;Item 3/3;Quit/Q');
  InLineP(AppendMenu, Menu[2], 'Object 1;Object 2;Object 3');
  InLineP(InsertMenu, Menu[1], 0);
  InLineP(InsertMenu, Menu[2], 0);
  InLineP(DrawMenuBar);
{**** Set boundary for moving window ****}
  SetRect(DragRect, 4, 24, 508, 338);
{**** Set the area to erase before printing ****}
  SetRect(Paper, 50, 50, 300, 300);
end;

procedure Terminate;
begin
{**** Get rid of our menus ****}
  InLineP(ClearMenuBar);
  InLineP(DisposeMenu, Menu[1]);
  InLineP(DisposeMenu, Menu[2]);
{**** Get rid of the window ****}
  InLineP(CloseWindow, DispWindow);
{**** Restore Macintosh Pascal's Menus ****}
  InLineP(SetMenuBar, OldMenuBar);
```

```
      InLineP(DrawMenuBar);
    end;

    procedure DrawLn (TextStr : Str255);
    begin
{**** Write a string in the middle of the window in the system font ****}
      EraseRect(Paper);
      MoveTo(100, 100);
      TextFont(0);
      DrawString(TextStr);
    end;

    procedure DoCommand (Result : Longint);
      var
        Temp : Boolean;
{**** Process a menu selection ****}
    begin
{**** Determine which menu was selected ****}
      case WInLineF(HiWord, Result) of
        ItemMenu :
{**** Determine which menu item from Item menu ****}
{**** Print Detail of selection ****}
          case WInLineF(LoWord, Result) of
            1 :
              DrawLn('Item 1 selected ');
            2 :
              DrawLn('Item 2 Selected');
            3 :
              DrawLn('Item 3 Selected');
            4 :
              Done := true;
          end;
        ObjectMenu :
{**** Determine which menu item from Object menu ****}
{**** Print detail of selection ****}
          case WInLineF(LoWord, Result) of
            1 :
              DrawLn('Object 1 selected ');
            2 :
              DrawLn('Object 2 Selected'),
            3 :
              DrawLn('Object 3 Selected');
          end;
        otherwise
          DrawLn('Nothing Selected');
      end;
{**** Unlight menu title once processing is complete ****}
      InLineP(HiliteMenu, 0);
      Temp := BInLineF(GetNextEvent, MouseUp, @Event);
    end;
    procedure TrackMouse;
      var
        Temp : Boolean;
```

```
  begin
    repeat
{**** Wait until an event occurs ****}
    repeat
    until BInLineF(GetNextEvent, EventMask, @Event);
{**** Determine type of event and process ****}
    case Event.what of
      MouseDown :
{**** Event is mouse button down - Determine where and process ****}
      case WInLineF(FindWindow, Event.where, @whichWindow) of
        InMenuBar :
          DoCommand(LInLineF(MenuSelect, Event.where));
        InDrag :
          InLineP(DragWindow, whichWindow, Event.where, DragRect);
        otherwise
          begin
            DrawLn('No Action Taken');
            repeat
            until BInLineF(GetNextEvent, MouseUpMask, @Event);
          end;
      end;
      KeyDown :
        DoCommand(LInLineF(MenuKey, chr(Event.message mod 256)));
      otherwise
        DrawLn('No Corresponding Menu Item');
    end;
  until Done = true;
end,

begin
{**** Main Loop ****}
  SetUp;
  TrackMouse;
  Terminate;
end.
```

This program begins by naming the constants to be used throughout the rest of the program. The trap locations, listed first, are divided into their respective managers. These trap locations are followed by manager constants—those values returned by manager functions to indicate a specific condition. For example, EventMask has bit 1 and bit 3 set (bits are a number from right to left starting with 0) to tell the Event Manager to look for mouse button down or key down events only. The last pair of constants gives the menus an arbitrary reference "name" for use by the Menu Manager.

The program begins with a call to procedure SetUp, which removes Macintosh Pascal's windows from the desktop and calls a procedure to initialize a new window. The remainder of SetUp stores and clears the Pascal menu bar and creates a new menu bar.

The next procedure, TrackMouse, again controls the operation of the program. TrackMouse waits for a key or mouse button down event to occur. If a key down event occurs, we use the MenuKey function to determine which menu and item were selected. Since the MenuKey function uses a character as its parameter, our program must determine which character was pressed. Fortunately, the Event Manager gives us this information in the Event.message field. This field is of type longint, making it four bytes long. After a key down event, the lowest byte contains the character code of the key pressed. This code depends upon the current configuration of the keyboard and upon whether any modifier keys were pressed as well. Normally, the code is the ASCII code for that key. The next highest byte contains the key code in case you want to use the keyboard for some unusual purpose, such as composing music. The remaining two bytes of this field are not used during a key down event. The expression

Event.message mod 256

conveniently returns the low-order byte of the message field that contains the character code.

If the event is a mouse button down event, there are two possible outcomes: either the user has selected a menu or wants to drag the window. By using the FindWindow function, the Window Manager tells the program where the mouse button down event occurred. Notice the address operator @ in the parameter list of the InLine function. If you go back to the definition of the FindWindow function, you will see that this second parameter is defined with the var statement and awaits the address of the variable. After you run the program a few times, remove the @ symbol. Run the program and first use the mouse and keyboard to select a few menu items. Then use the mouse to drag the window. As soon as you press the mouse button in the title bar, you will get a system error. This means that the FindWindow function does not use the second parameter at all when the event is related to the menu bar. When writing programs using the InLine routines, be aware that a routine may work properly under one or more conditions but may cause a system error under another condition. This kind of bug is extremely difficult to find.

Once we have determined the location of the mouse button down event, it can be processed by the respective manager functions, either MenuSelect or DragWindow.

The DoCommand procedure takes the longint result from the MenuSelect or MenuKey function and processes it to perform the appropriate menu selection. If the Quit option is chosen, the global variable Done is set to True, which causes the TrackMouse function to terminate.

Finally, the program calls procedure Terminate, which removes the menus and window and restores the regular Pascal menu bar.

Some Final Notes

At this point, you can take the basic program and enhance it. You may want to start by working with the Menu Manager routines because they are less complicated. Try adding new menus with options that disable and enable other menu items. You may begin by removing the ClearMenuBar call in SetUp and see what effect your menus have on the Pascal menu bar.

Despite this head start, you will find working with windows quite complex. For example, remove the HideAll statement from SetUp and drag the window around the screen. You will notice that it erases what is underneath it. Unfortunately, there is no convenient way to redraw these newly visible regions from Macintosh Pascal. If you want to use your own windows, you may not want to allow the user to move or resize the window unless it is the only window on the desktop. Instead, you may have two or four windows set on the screen and allow the user to move from window to window using the appropriate functions.

Summary

This chapter explained how to use the four Inline routines, InlineP, BInlineF, WInlineF, and LInlineF, to gain access to the Macintosh Toolbox. It showed that using only these four routines makes it possible to implement all of the procedures and functions stored in the Toolbox. To use them, however, you must incorporate the trap numbers associated with each routine you want to call in your program.

Two of the most important managers contained in the Toolbox were examined in detail. In the section about the Menu Manager, techniques were explained for initializing and using these routines to create your own menus. These menus can be used in the same way that a complete Macintosh application uses its menus.

Windows and their uses were discussed in the section about the Window Manager. Using a window to exploit its utmost potential requires many different routines. The Macintosh Toolbox, particularly the Window Manager, provide procedures and functions to handle the multitude of events that occur during window processing. The effective use of these procedures and functions can give your programs sophistication and elegance.

APPENDIX

A Reference Guide

Even after you become familiar with Macintosh programming, you may occasionally require assistance with a procedure, function, or data type. The following reference guide has been designed to provide rapid answers to questions concerning Macintosh Pascal.

The guide is divided into thirteen sections, each section dealing with one specific area of specialization (such as data types and QuickDraw Calculation Procedures). To use this guide, simply find the appropriate section, then read down the summary list to find the desired item. The syntax of the procedure or function is given if required, followed by a brief description of its use. An example of how to use the operation is sometimes provided when the meaning of the operation's use is not completely clear. The thirteen sections are presented in the following order:

Bit Transfer Procedures

Cursor Control Procedures

Menu Manager Routines

Miscellaneous QuickDraw Routines

Mouse Control Routines

Pen Control Procedures

Picture Routines

QuickDraw Calculation Routines

QuickDraw Data Types

QuickDraw Graphics Procedures

Text Control Procedures

Window Manager Functions

Window Manipulation Procedures

Bit Transfer Procedures

These procedures are used to transfer bit images between different bit maps. The bit transfer procedures are presented in the following sequence:

CopyBits

ScrollRect

procedure CopyBits (srcBits, dstBits:BitMap; srcRect, dstRect:Rect; mode:integer; maskRgn:RgnHandle);

The CopyBits procedure transfers the bit image bounded by srcRect from the srcBits bit map to the bit image bounded by dstRect in the dstBits bitmap. The transfer mode is specified by mode, and the resulting bit image is clipped by the region pointed to by maskRgn.

The transfer mode may be one of the following eight modes:

srcCopy	srcXor	notSrcCopy	notSrcXor
srcOr	srcBic	notSrcOr	notSrcBic

If nil is passed as the maskRgn parameter, no clipping of the destination bit image takes place. The srcRect rectangle will always be completely aligned with the dstRect rectangle. If the two rectangles are of different sizes, the source bit image will be resized (shrunk or expanded) as necessary to fit the bit image enclosed by the dstRect rectangle.

The coordinate plane of srcBits defined by srcBits.bounds is used as the basis for srcRect, and the coordinate plane of dstBits defined by dstBits.bounds is used as the basis for dstRect and maskRgn.

Figure A-1 illustrates an example of the operation of the CopyBits procedure.

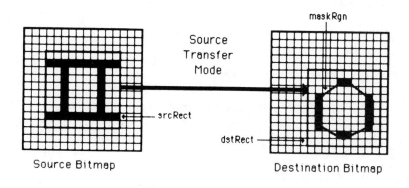

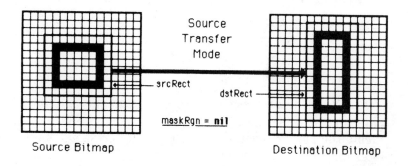

Figure A-1. CopyBits example

procedure ScrollRect (r:Rect; dh, dv:integer;
updateRgn:RgnHandle);

The ScrollRect procedure shifts the bits inside the intersection of the rectangle specified by r, VisRgn, clipRgn, portRect, and portBits.bounds. The bits are shifted horizontally by the distance specified in dh and vertically by the distance specified by dv. If dh and dv are positive, the direction of movement is to the right and down. If dh and dv are negative, the direction of movement is to the left and up. Bits outside the scroll intersection area are not affected, because bits shifted outside the scroll area are lost. The space created by the shift inside the scroll area will be filled with the current grafPort's background pattern. The region pointed to by updateRgn will be set to the area filled with the background pattern. The pen location is not changed by ScrollRect, although it will change relative to the shifted area. Figure A-2 shows an example of the effects of ScrollRect.

Cursor Control Procedures

These procedures are used to control the cursor that is connected to the mouse. The five cursor control procedures are presented in the following sequence:

HideCursor

InitCursor

ObscureCursor

SetCursor

ShowCursor

procedure HideCursor;

The HideCursor procedure removes the cursor from the screen, allowing the bits under it to become visible. HideCursor also decrements the cursor level. Calls to HideCursor should be balanced by later calls to ShowCursor.

procedure InitCursor;

The InitCursor procedure initializes the cursor to a predefined

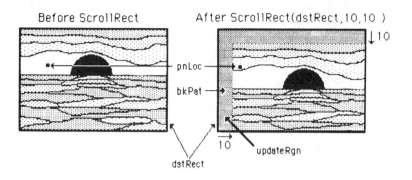

Before ScrollRect   After ScrollRect(dstRect,10,10)

pnLoc

bkPat

updateRgn

dstRect

Figure A-2. ScrollRect example

arrow pointing north-northwest and sets the cursor level to 0. The cursor level is used to keep track of repeated calls to HideCursor and ShowCursor. The cursor level is set to 0 when the Macintosh is started.

procedure ObscureCursor;

ObscureCursor hides the cursor until the mouse is moved. It has no effect on the cursor level and need not be balanced by a call to ShowCursor.

procedure SetCursor (crsr:Cursor);

The SetCursor procedure defines the cursor as the 16 × 16 bit image in crsr. If the cursor is visible, it immediately changes to the image defined in crsr. If the cursor is hidden, however, it takes on its new appearance when uncovered.

procedure ShowCursor;

ShowCursor negates the effects of a previous call to HideCursor, making the cursor visible on the screen and incrementing the cursor level. Extraneous calls to ShowCursor when the cursor is already visible have no effect. If there has been a prior call to SetCursor while the cursor was hidden, ShowCursor presents the new cursor.

Menu Manager Routines

There are 16 routines in this category. They are presented in the following order:

AppendMenu

CheckItem

ClearMenuBar

DeleteMenu

DisableItem

DrawMenuBar

EnableItem

GetItemStyle

GetMenuBar

HiliteMenu

InsertMenu

MenuKey

MenuSelect

NewMenu

SetItemStyle

SetMenuBar

**procedure AppendMenu (theMenu:MenuHandle;
data:Str255);**

AppendMenu adds an item or items to the end of the menu specified by theMenu. The data string may be blank but should not be null. This string contains the text of the item or items that you wish to append to the menu. Special metacharacters may be used:

Metacharacter	Meaning
; or Return	Separates multiple items.
^	Followed by an icon number, adds that icon to the item.
!	Followed by a character, marks that item with that character.
<	Followed by B, I, U, O, or S, sets the character style of the item.

/	Followed by a character, associates a keyboard equivalent with that item.
(	Disables the item.

procedure CheckItem (menu:MenuHandle; item:integer; checked:boolean);

When CheckItem is called (with checked set to True), a check mark will appear next to the specified item number in the menu pointed to by menu. To reverse the effect—to remove the check mark from an item—call the procedure with checked set to False, item set to the item number, and menu set to the menuhandle of the menu in which the item resides.

procedure ClearMenuBar;

ClearMenuBar deletes all of the menus in the current menu bar, allowing the programmer to start afresh and create a completely new menu list.

procedure DeleteMenu (menuID:integer);

The menu identified by menuID will be deleted from the menu list. If there is no menu with the specified ID, the procedure has no effect.

procedure DisableItem (theMenu:MenuHandle; item:integer);

DisableItem disables the menu item specified by item in the menu pointed to by theMenu. If item is set to 0, the entire menu is disabled. If the entire menu is disabled, the menu title appears dimmed, but it is necessary to call DrawMenuBar to display the dimmed menu title.

procedure DrawMenuBar;

DrawMenuBar redraws the menu bar, incorporating any changes that have been made since the last time the menu bar was drawn. This procedure is always called after invoking any procedure that makes any changes to the menu list. The new menu list will not become active until this procedure is called.

procedure EnableItem (theMenu:MenuHandle; item:integer);

EnableItem enables the item number specified by item in the menu indicated by theMenu. If item is set to 0, the entire menu is enabled. As with DisableItem, it is necessary to call DrawMenuBar to display the new appearance of the menu title.

procedure GetItemStyle (theMenu:MenuHandle; item:integer; var chStyle:Style);

GetItemStyle is used to interrogate a menu item's character style.

function GetMenuBar:Handle;

GetMenuBar saves a copy of the current menu list. This allows for the use of new menu lists (or for the modification of the current menu list) and then to return to the current menu (the one now being saved). An old menu may be recalled at any time by using the SetMenuBar procedure. This function returns a handle to reference the copy of the menu list that has been stored.

procedure HiliteMenu (menuID:integer);

HiliteMenu highlights the menu title specified by menuID. This procedure has no effect if the title is already highlighted. If the menuID is set to 0 or is a menuID that does not exist in the menu list, any menu that is highlighted will be unhighlighted. To reverse the effects of MenuSelect or MenuKey on the menu title, call this procedure when an applications program completes processing a menu selection.

procedure InsertMenu (theMenu:MenuHandle; beforeID:integer);

InsertMenu forms the menu list by inserting the handle of the menu defined by theMenu before the menu whose menu ID is defined by beforeID. If beforeID is set to 0, the new menu is added after the last menu in the list. Remember to use DrawMenuBar to update the menu bar.

function MenuKey (ch:char):longint;

MenuKey is called when a key press occurs with the COMMAND key held down. The character typed is passed to the MenuKey function in the ch parameter. The MenuKey function returns the result as if the item had been selected from a menu by using the mouse, and it highlights the menu title of the menu in the same way as

MenuSelect. After processing the result of MenuKey, it is necessary to call HiliteMenu(0) to remove the menu title's highlighting.

If no item in any menu possesses the COMMAND key equivalent, MenuKey returns 0.

function MenuSelect (startPt:Point):longint;

During a menu selection, MenuSelect performs the necessary menu management routines. The startPt parameter should be set to the point at which the mouse button down event occurs (the where field from the event record). The MenuSelect function tracks the mouse, pulls down the menus as required, and highlights the menu items as the mouse moves over them. When the mouse button is released, the MenuSelect function returns two integers in the high- and low-order words of the long integer. The high word contains the menuID of the menu in which the final selection occurred. The low word contains the item number of the final selection. Items are numbered from the top to the bottom of the menu, starting with 1.

After a selection is made, the MenuSelect function blinks the item selected, releases the menu, and highlights the menu title. When the applications program completes processing the selection, it calls the HiliteMenu procedure with menuID set to 0 to clear the highlighting from the menuTitle.

If no selection is made, MenuSelect returns to 0.

function NewMenu (menuID:integer;
menuTitle:Str255):MenuHandle;

NewMenu is used to inform the Menu Manager that you want the space for a new menu. The new menu will have the ID menuID and the title menuTitle. The new menu is created empty. Therefore, you should use AppendMenu to fill the menu with the items you want. The menu ID should be a positive integer greater than 0.

procedure SetItemStyle (theMenu:MenuHandle;
item:integer; chStyle:Style);

SetItemStyle is used to change the character style of a menu item's appearance.

procedure SetMenuBar (menuList:Handle);

This procedure reinstates the menu list pointed to by menuList as the current menu.

Miscellaneous QuickDraw Routines

This category is composed of eight QuickDraw routines, which are presented in the following order:

GetPixel

MapPoly

MapPt

MapRect

MapRgn

Random

ScalePt

StuffHex

function GetPixel (h, v:integer):boolean;

Function GetPixel examines the pixel at the coordinates specified by h and v. GetPixel returns True if the pixel is black and False if the pixel is white. GetPixel will return the status of the coordinate specified, even if the point does not exist within the current graf-Port. To determine whether or not the point belongs to the current grafPort, use PtInRgn.

procedure MapPoly (poly:PolyHandle; srcRect, dstRect:Rect);

Given a polygon within srcRect, MapPoly maps it to a similarly located polygon within dstRect. MapPoly uses MapPt to map all the points that define the polygon.

procedure MapPt (var pt:Point; srcRect, dstRect:Rect);

Given a point within srcRect, MapPt places it into a similarly located point within dstRect. In locating the position of the destination rectangle, MapPt expands or contracts the source to fit within the destination. The result is returned in pt.

procedure MapRect (var r:Rect; srcRect, dstRect:Rect);

Given a rectangle within srcRect, MapRect maps it to a similarly located rectangle within dstRect. It calls MapPt to map the upper left and lower right corners of the rectangle. The result of the mapping is returned in r.

procedure MapRgn (rgn:RgnHandle; srcRect, dstRect:Rect);

Given a region within srcRect, MapRgn maps it to a similarly located region within dstRect. It calls MapPt to map all the points within the region.

function Random:integer;

Like any good random number generator, the Random function returns an integer between −32768 and +32767. The sequence of values returned depends upon the value of global variable RandSeed, which InitGraf sets to 1. Should you want to perform the sequence again from the beginning, simply reset RandSeed to 1.

procedure ScalePt (var pt:Point; srcRect, dstRect:Rect);

The width and height are passed in pt. The horizontal component is the width and the vertical component is the height. ScalePt manipulates these measurements as follows and returns the result in pt: ScalePt multiplies the given width by the ratio of dstRect's width to srcRect's width and multiplies the given height by the ratio of dstRect's height to srcRect's height.

procedure StuffHex (thingPtr:QDPtr; s:Str255);

StuffHex pokes bits into a data structure. The bits are expressed as a string of hexadecimal digits. Using StuffHex is great for creating cursors, patterns, or other bit images that can later be pushed onto the screen using CopyBits.

There is no range testing performed on the size of the destination variable. Therefore, it's up to the programmer to ensure that there is enough space on the receiving side of the destination variable. If you are not careful, you can easily overrun the size of the variable and destroy the contents of some unknown location in memory.

Mouse Control Routines

This section describes the procedures and functions used to determine the mouse status. The four routines are presented in the following sequence:

Button

GetMouse

StillDown

WaitMouseUp

function Button:boolean;

Button is a Boolean procedure that returns True if the mouse button is currently held down and False if the button isn't being held down.

procedure GetMouse (var x,y:integer);

GetMouse returns the current location of the cursor hotspot, with the variable x equivalent to the Point.v coordinate and the variable y equivalent to the Point.h coordinate. A returned negative value indicates that the hotspot is outside the drawing window.

function StillDown:boolean;

StillDown is a Boolean function that returns True if the mouse button has been held down continuously since the last mouse event inquiry.

function WaitMouseUp:boolean;

WaitMouseUp returns True if the mouse button has been held down since the last mouse event inquiry. If the mouse button has been released, the mouse up event is removed from the event queue.

Pen Control Procedures

The pen control procedures are used to control the various features of the graphics pen used for drawing operations by QuickDraw. Each grafPort has one pen. This section also covers procedures used to both move the pen around the grafPort and to draw lines. The 13 items are presented in the following sequence:

GetPen

GetPenState

HidePen

Line

LineTo

Move

MoveTo

PenMode

PenNormal

PenPat

PenSize

SetPenState

ShowPen

procedure GetPen (var pt:Point);

The GetPen procedure returns the current pen location in pt. The location returned is in the local coordinates of the current grafPort.

procedure GetPenState (var pnState:PenState);

The GetPenState procedure uses the variable pnState to save the pen location, size, pattern, and mode. The pen state may be restored with a later call to SetPenState. This is a handy procedure that can be used when calling short subroutines that operate in the current grafPort but that must change the attributes of the graphics pen.

procedure HidePen;

The HidePen procedure has the effect of preventing the graphics pen from drawing on the screen. It decrements the grafPort's pnVis field (initialized to 0 by OpenPort). If pnVis is negative, the pen will not draw on the screen. PnVis is used in a manner similar to the cursor level, compensating for repeated calls to HidePen and ShowPen. OpenRgn, OpenPicture, and OpenPoly all call HidePen so that regions, pictures, and polygons may be created without affecting the screen.

procedure Line (dh, dv:integer);

The Line procedure draws a line from the current pen location to the location that is specified by dh horizontally and dv vertically. The pen ends up at the position that is specified by (h + dh, v + dv). If dh and dv are positive, the movement is to the right and down. If dh and dv are negative, the movement is to the left and up.

procedure LineTo (h, v:integer);

The LineTo procedure draws a line from the current pen location to the location specified by h and v in the coordinates of the current grafPort. The pen ends up at the location specified by (h,v). If a region definition or polygon structure is open, a call to LineTo will mathematically add the line to the region or polygon being formed.

procedure Move (h, v:integer);

Without drawing on the screen, the Move procedure moves the pen from its current location horizontally by the distance specified in h and vertically by the distance specified by v. If h and v are positive, the movement is to the right and down. If h and v are negative, the movement is to the left and up.

procedure MoveTo (h, v:integer);

Without drawing on the screen, the MoveTo procedure moves the graphics pen to the location specified by (h,v) in the local coordinates of the current grafPort.

procedure PenMode (mode:integer);

The PenMode procedure is used to define the transfer mode by which a pattern is transferred to the bit map when graphics drawing takes place. The mode may be any one of the following pattern transfer modes:

patCopy	patXor	notPatCopy	notPatXor
patOr	patBic	notPatOr	notPatBic

If the mode is a source transfer mode or is negative, no drawing takes place. The field pnMode contains the current pen mode, which is initially set to patCopy.

procedure PenNormal;

The PenNormal procedure is used to initialize or reset the initial state of the pen in the current grafPort. PenNormal sets pensize to (1,1), pnMode to PatCopy, and pnPat to black. The pen's location is not changed.

procedure PenPat (pat:Pattern);

The PenPat procedure is used to set the pattern used by the pen in the current grafPort. The constants white, black, light gray, and dark gray may be used to set the respective predefined pen patterns. The field pnPat contains the current grafPort's pen pattern, which is initialized to black.

procedure PenSize (width, height:integer);

The PenSize procedure sets the dimensions of the graphics pen in the current grafPort to the specified width and height. Subsequent calls to graphics procedures that use the graphics pen utilize the new pen dimensions. The field pnSize, which is of type Point, contains the current pen dimensions. If either of the pen dimensions becomes negative, the pen assumes the dimensions (0,0) and no drawing is performed.

procedure SetPenState (pnState:PenState);

The SetPenState procedure sets the pen location, size, pattern, and mode of the graphics pen of the current grafPort to the values stored in pnState.

procedure ShowPen;

The ShowPen procedure has the effect of allowing the graphics pen to draw graphics images on the screen. ShowPen increments the current grafPort's pnVis field, which may have been previously decremented by HidePen. As soon as pnVis becomes equal to 0, QuickDraw commences drawing on the screen. CloseRgn, ClosePicture, and ClosePoly all call ShowPen to balance the calls to HidePen made by OpenRgn, OpenPicture, and OpenPoly.

Picture Routines

Pictures are formed from a transcript of calls to QuickDraw routines. When completed, they may be manipulated as single graphics objects by the following routines. The five routines are arranged in the following sequence:

ClosePicture

DrawPicture

KillPicture

OpenPicture

PicComment

procedure ClosePicture;

ClosePicture completes the formation of a picture, telling Quick-Draw to stop saving function calls and picture comments. ClosePicture calls ShowPen to balance OpenPicture's call to HidePen.

procedure DrawPicture (myPicture:PicHandle; dstRect:Rect);

This procedure draws the given picture to scale in dstRect, expanding or contracting it as necessary to align the borders of the picture frame with dstRect.

procedure KillPicture (myPicture:PicHandle);

Procedure KillPicture clears the memory required to store the picture defined by the handle specified in PicHandle. The memory occupied by the picture is returned to the free memory pool.

function OpenPicture (picFrame:Rect):picHandle;

Used to start a picture definition, OpenPicture returns a handle to the new picture, which is drawn within the rectangle specified by picFrame. Subsequent calls to drawing procedures and picture comments will be saved as part of the picture definition. OpenPicture calls the procedure HidePen, preventing calls to graphics procedures from drawing upon the screen. A call to ShowPen after the call to OpenPicture will allow drawing to occur. While a picture is open, the current grafPort's picSave field contains a handle to the information about the picture. In order to temporarily disable the formation of a picture, this field may be saved and set to nil. Later restoration of the field reenables picture formation.

procedure PicComment (kind, dataSize:integer;
dataHandle:QDHandle);

PicComment writes the specified text into the definition of the currently opened picture. Additional data is sent to the procedure through dataHandle, where dataSize is the size of the data in bytes. If there is no additional data for the comment, dataHandle should be nil and dataSize should be 0. The surrounding program that processes the picture comments must include a procedure to process and store a pointer according to the procedure in the data structure pointed to by the grafProcs field in the grafPort.

QuickDraw Calculation Routines

This section details all of the routines available to perform various calculations on the different graphics objects that may be manipulated by QuickDraw. Calculations do not normally affect the screen, but are utilized prior to calling one of the QuickDraw graphics routines. The 38 routines are arranged in the following order:

AddPt

ClosePoly

CloseRgn

CopyRgn

DiffRgn

DisposeRgn

EmptyRect

EmptyRgn

EqualPt

EqualRect

EqualRgn

GlobalToLocal

InsetRect

InsetRgn

KillPoly

LocalToGlobal

NewRgn

OffsetPoly

OffsetRect

OffsetRgn

OpenPoly

OpenRgn

Pt2Rect

PtInRect

PtInRgn

PtToAngle

RectInRgn

RectRgn

SectRect

SectRgn

SetEmptyRgn

SetPt

SetRect

SetRectRgn

SubPt

UnionRect

UnionRgn

XorRgn

procedure AddPt (srcPt:Point; var dstPt:Point);

AddPt adds the coordinates defined by srcPt and dstPt and returns the result in dstPt.

procedure ClosePoly;

ClosePoly completes the polygon definition initiated by OpenPoly, organizes the collection of lines into a polygon definition, and computes the PolyBox rectangle. Only one ClosePoly call should be performed for each call to OpenPoly. ClosePoly calls ShowPen to balance OpenPoly's call to HidePen.

procedure CloseRgn (dstRgn:RgnHandle);

CloseRgn completes the region definition initiated by OpenRgn by organizing the collection of lines and framed shapes into a region definition. It then saves the resulting region into the structure pointed to by dstRgn. Only one call to CloseRgn should be performed for each call to OpenRgn. CloseRgn calls ShowPen to balance OpenRgn's call to HidePen.

procedure CopyRgn (srcRgn, dstRgn:RgnHandle);

CopyRgn makes a duplicate copy of srcRgn in dstRgn. NewRgn must be called prior to calling CopyRgn to initialize dstRgn and reserve the memory required on Macintosh's heap.

procedure DiffRgn (srcRgnA, srcRgnB, dstRgn:RgnHandle);

DiffRgn subtracts the region pointed to by srcRgnB from the region pointed to by srcRgnA and places the result into the region pointed to by dstRgn. If the region pointed to by srcRgnA is empty, the region pointed to by dstRgn is set to the empty region (0,0,0,0). DiffRgn does not create the region pointed to by dstRgn. While dstRgn may be set to one of the source regions, if it is a separate region it is necessary to call NewRgn to create the region pointed to by dstRgn prior to calling DiffRgn.

procedure DisposeRgn (rgn:RgnHandle);

DisposeRgn deallocates the space previously used for the region definition rgn. The memory is returned to the free memory pool. The contents of a region are not recoverable once this procedure has been called for a region.

function EmptyRect (r:Rect):boolean;

EmptyRect returns True if the rectangle r is an empty rectangle (0,0,0,0). A rectangle is considered empty if the bottom coordinate is equal to or less than the top coordinate or if the right coordinate is equal to or less than the left coordinate.

function EmptyRgn (rgn:RgnHandle):boolean;

EmptyRgn returns True if the region pointed to by rgn is an empty region.

function EqualPt (ptA, ptB:Point):boolean;

EqualPt compares the points ptA and ptB and returns True if they are equal. Otherwise, False is returned.

function EqualRect (rectA, rectB:Rect):boolean;

EqualRect returns True if the two source rectangles rectA and rectB are equal. The two rectangles must have identical boundary coordinates to be considered equal.

function EqualRgn (rgnA, rgnB:RgnHandle):boolean;

EqualRgn returns True if the two source regions pointed to by srcRgnA and srcRgnB are equal. The two regions must have identical sizes, shapes, and locations to be considered equal.

procedure GlobalToLocal (var pt:Point);

GlobalToLocal converts the point pt, expressed as a global coordinate, with the upper left corner of the bit map as (0,0), to the local coordinates of the current grafPort.

procedure InsetRect (var r:Rect; dh, dv:integer);

InsetRect shrinks or expands the rectangle defined by r. The left and right sides are moved in if positive or out if negative, by the quantity specified in dh. The top and bottom are moved in or out (depending on positive or negative, respectively) by the amount specified in dv. If the width or height become less than 1, the rectangle returned is the empty rectangle, (0,0,0,0).

procedure InsetRgn (rgn:RgnHandle; dh, dv:integer);

Similar to InsetRect, InsetRgn shrinks or expands the region pointed to by rgn horizontally by the distance specified in dh and vertically by the distance specified in dv. If dh and dv are positive, the points defining the region are moved inward. If they are negative, the points defining the region are moved outward. The region will remain centered at its current position and will not affect the screen until a subsequent call to a procedure that draws the region.

procedure KillPoly (poly:PolyHandle);

KillPoly deallocates space for the polygon whose handle is defined by poly. It returns the memory used by the polygon definition to the free memory pool.

procedure LocalToGlobal (var pt:Point);

LocalToGlobal converts the point pt from the current grafPort's local coordinate system to a point with the origin at (0,0) at the upper left corner of the port's bit image. This global point can then be compared with other global points or changed into the local coordinates of another grafPort.

function NewRgn:RgnHandle;

NewRgn allocates space on the Macintosh heap for a new, dynamic, variable-sized region. It is initialized to the empty region (0,0,0,0) and returns a handle to the new region.

procedure OffsetPoly (poly:PolyHandle; dh, dv:integer);

Similar to OffsetRect, OffsetPoly moves the polygon pointed to by poly horizontally on the coordinate plane by the distance specified in dh and vertically by the distance specified by dv. If dh and dv are positive, the movement is to the right and down. If they are negative, the movement is to the left and up. OffsetPoly does not affect the screen until a subsequent call to a procedure to draw the polygon, nor does it affect the size and shape of the polygon.

procedure OffsetRect (var r:Rect; dh, dv:integer);

OffSetRect moves the rectangle defined by r. It adds dv to the vertical coordinates and dh to the horizontal coordinates. The corresponding movement is to the right and down if dh and dv are positive, and to the left and up if dh and dv are negative.

procedure OffsetRgn (rgn:RgnHandle; dh, dv:integer);

Similar to OffsetRect, OffsetRgn moves the region pointed to by rgn horizontally on the coordinate plane by the distance specified by dh and vertically by the distance specified by dv. If dh and dv are positive, the movement is to the right and down. If they are negative, the movement is to the left and up. OffsetRgn does not affect the screen until a subsequent call to draw the region, nor does it affect the size and shape of the region.

function OpenPoly:PolyHandle;

OpenPoly initiates the construction of a polygon definition. It allocates temporary space on Macintosh's heap to hold the polygon definition and calls the routine HidePen to prevent further calls to graphics operations from drawing on the screen. While the polygon is open, all calls to Line and LineTo are mathematically added to the outline of the polygon. Only the line end points will affect the polygon definition. A polygon should consist of a closed loop.

procedure OpenRgn;

OpenRgn initiates the construction of a region definition. It allocates temporary space on Macintosh's heap to hold the region definition and calls the routine HidePen to prevent further calls to graphics operations from drawing on the screen. While the region is open, all calls to MoveTo, Line, LineTo, and the procedures that draw framed shapes (except arcs) affect the outline of the region. Only the line end points and shape boundaries affect the region definition. A region should consist of one or more closed loops. Each framed shape is itself a closed loop.

procedure Pt2Rect (ptA, ptB:Point; var dstRect:Rect);

Pt2Rect returns the smallest rectangle in dstRect that encloses the two input points ptA and ptB.

function PtInRect (pt:Point; r:Rect):boolean;

PtInRect returns True if the pixel below and to the right of the given coordinate point pt is enclosed within the rectangle specified by r.

function PtInRgn (pt:Point; rgn:RgnHandle):boolean;

PtInRgn returns True if the pixel below and to the right of the given coordinate point pt is enclosed within the region pointed to by rgn.

procedure PtToAngle (r:Rect; pt:Point; var angle:integer);

PtToAngle returns the integer angle in degrees in variable angle between a line from the center of the rectangle straight up (12 o'clock) and a line from the center of the rectangle to the given point pt. The angle returned is measured clockwise from the vertical line.

If the line to the given point passes through the upper right corner of the rectangle, the angle returned is 45 degrees. The value of 45 is returned even if the rectangle is not a square. If the line passes through the lower right corner of the rectangle, the angle returned is 135 degrees, and so on.

function RectInRgn (r:Rect; rgn:RgnHandle):boolean;

RectInRgn returns True if the rectangle r intersects the region pointed to by rgn and at least one bit is enclosed.

procedure RectRgn (rgn:RgnHandle; r:Rect);

Similar to SetRectRgn, this procedure destroys the structure pointed to by rgn and replaces it with the rectangle specified by r. The difference between RectRgn and SetRectRgn is that the input rectangle in RectRgn is defined by a rectangle, rather than by the four boundary coordinates defined in SetRectRgn.

function SectRect (srcRectA, srcRectB:Rect; var dstRect:Rect):boolean;

SectRect calculates the rectangle that is the intersection of the two source rectangles srcRectA and srcRectB. It returns True if they intersect and False if they don't. Touching rectangles are not considered to intersect. If the rectangles do not intersect, the destination rectangle dstRect is set to the empty rectangle (0,0,0,0).

procedure SectRgn (srcRgnA, srcRgnB, dstRgn:RgnHandle);

Like SectRect, SectRgn calculates the intersection of the two regions pointed to by srcRgnA and srcRgnB. The procedure places the result into the region pointed to by dstRgn. If the regions do not intersect, or if one of the regions contains an empty region, dstRgn is set to the empty region (0,0,0,0). SectRgn does not create the region pointed to by dstRgn. While dstRgn may be set to point at one of the source regions, if it is a separate region it is necessary to call NewRgn to create the region pointed to by dstRgn prior to calling SectRgn.

procedure SetEmptyRgn (rgn:RgnHandle);

SetEmptyRgn destroys the structure of the region definition pointed to by rgn and replaces it with the empty region (0,0,0,0).

procedure SetPt (var pt:Point; h, v:integer);

SetPt assigns the two integer coordinates h and v to the point pt.

procedure SetRect (var r:Rect; left, top, right, bottom:integer);

SetRect returns the variable r set to the four boundary coordinates of a rectangle: left, top, right, and bottom.

procedure SetRectRgn (rgn:RgnHandle; left, top, right, bottom:integer);

SetRectRgn destroys the structure of the region pointed to by rgn and then sets the new structure to the rectangle specified by left, top, right, and bottom. If the specified rectangle is empty, the structure is set to the empty region (0,0,0,0).

procedure SubPt (srcPt:Point; var dstPt:Point);

SubPt subtracts the coordinates specified by srcPt from dstPt and returns the result in dstPt.

procedure UnionRect (srcRectA, srcRectB:Rect; var dstRect:Rect);

UnionRect calculates the smallest rectangle that encloses both the source rectangles srcRectA and srcRectB and returns the result in dstRect.

procedure UnionRgn (srcRgnA, srcRgnB, dstRgn:RgnHandle);

Similar to UnionRect, UnionRgn calculates the union of the two regions pointed to by srcRgnA and srcRgnB and places the result into the region pointed to by dstRgn. If both regions are empty, the destination region is set to the empty region (0,0,0,0). UnionRgn does not create dstRgn. While dstRgn may be set to one of the source regions, it is necessary to call NewRgn to create dstRgn prior to calling UnionRgn, if it is a separate region.

procedure XorRgn (srcRgnA, srcRgnB, dstRgn:RgnHandle);

XorRgn calculates the difference between the union and the intersection of the region pointed to by srcRgnA and the region pointed to by srcRgnB and places the result into the region pointed to by dstRgn. If the regions are coincident, the region pointed to by dstRgn is set to the empty region (0,0,0,0). XorRgn does not create dstRgn. While dstRgn may be set to one of the source regions, if it is a separate region it is necessary to call NewRgn to create the region pointed to by dstRgn prior to calling XorRgn.

QuickDraw Data Types

This section describes the various data types and structures used in parameters and variables throughout QuickDraw procedures and functions. The 18 data types are presented in the following sequence:

BitMap

Cursor

Pattern

PicHandle

PicPtr

Picture

Point

PolyHandle

PolyPtr

Polygon

QDByte

QDHandle

QDPtr

Rect

Region

RgnHandle

RgnPtr

Style

BitMap

The data type BitMap is used by QuickDraw to impose a coordinate system to an area of memory that contains a bit image. It is defined as

```
type BitMap = record
         baseAddr:   QDPtr;
         rowBytes:   integer;
         bounds:     Rect;
     end;
```

where baseAddr is a pointer to the beginning of the image in memory, and the rowBytes field defines the number of bytes in each row of the image. The bounds field defines a rectangle that imposes the coordinate system on the bit image.

Cursor

The data type Cursor is used by QuickDraw to define a 256-bit image organized as a 16×16 rectangle. It defines the shape of the cursor controlled by the mouse. It is defined as

```
type Cursor = record
         data:      array [0..15] of integer;
         mask:      array [0..15] of integer;
         hotspot:   Point;
     end;
```

The data field contains the bit image of the cursor itself, while the mask field is used by QuickDraw to determine both the screen appearance of each bit of the cursor and the bits under the cursor that are already on the screen. Hotspot aligns the cursor with the position of the mouse. The following table shows Quickdraw's use of the mask and data fields to produce the final screen appearance of the cursor:

Data	Mask	Resulting Pixel on the Screen
0	1	White
1	1	Black
0	0	Same as pixel under cursor
1	0	Inverse of pixel under cursor

Pattern

The data type pattern is used by QuickDraw to define a 64-bit image organized as an 8 × 8 rectangle that defines the tone of the repeating pattern. It is defined as

type Pattern = packed array [0..7] of 0..255;

PicHandle

The data type PicHandle is defined as

type PicHandle = ^PicPtr;

PicHandle is used by QuickDraw to implement Macintosh's double-indirection method of memory management.

PicPtr

The data type PicPtr is used to point at the area of memory that contains the variable-length picture data. It is defined as

type PicPtr = ^Picture;

Picture

The data type Picture is used by QuickDraw to maintain a transcript of calls to routines that draw any picture on the bit map. It is used by QuickDraw to "replay" the sequence of commands that were originally used to draw the image. It is a variable-length structure and is defined as

```
type Picture = record
          picSize:      integer;
          picFrame:    Rect;
          {picture definition data}
     end;
```

The picSize field contains the size in bytes of the picture variable. The picFrame field defines a rectangle that completely encloses the picture. PicFrame is used for scaling by routines that redraw the picture.

Point

A data type of Point defines the intersection of horizontal and vertical grid lines on the QuickDraw coordinate plane. The data type of Point is defined as

```
type VHSelect = (V,H);
         Point = record case integer of
                      0:   (v:    integer;
                            h:    integer);
                      1:   (vh:   array [VHSelect] of integer)
         end;
```

PolyHandle

The data type PolyHandle is defined as

```
type PolyHandle = ^PolyPtr;
```

PolyHandle is used by QuickDraw to implement Macintosh's double-indirection method of memory management.

PolyPtr

The data type PolyPtr is used to point at the area of memory that contains the variable-length polygon data. It is defined as

```
type PolyPtr = ^Polygon;
```

Polygon

The data type polygon is used by QuickDraw to maintain the array of points used by QuickDraw to construct a polygon. It is a variable-length structure and is defined as

```
type Polygon = record
         polySize:      integer;
         polyBBox:      Rect;
         polyPoints:    array [0..0] of Point;
     end;
```

The polySize field contains the size in bytes of the polygon variable. The polyBBox field defines a rectangle that encloses the polygon. The array polyPoints will expand as necessary to contain the points in the polygon.

QDByte

The data type QDByte is one of three general data types. It is used to define the 8-bit byte as

type QDByte = −128..127;

where QDByte ranges in values from −128 and +127, inclusive.

QDHandle

The data type QDHandle is a QuickDraw general data type. It is used by QuickDraw to implement the Macintosh's double-indirection method of memory management. It is defined as

type QDHandle = ^QDPtr;

QDPtr

The data type QDPtr is another of QuickDraw's general data types. It is used to define a pointer to a contiguous area of memory on the Macintosh's heap. It is defined as

type QDPtr = ^QDByte;

Rect

The data type Rect defines both the upper left and the lower right points used by QuickDraw to construct a rectangle. It is defined as

```
type Rect = record case integer of
        0:    (top:           integer;
               left:          integer;
               bottom:        integer;
               right:         integer);

        1:    (topleft:       Point;
               botright:      Point);
    end;
```

Region

The data type Region consists of an arbitrary set of spatially related, coherent points used by QuickDraw to define a region. It is a variable-length type defined as

```
type Region = record
        rgnSize:        integer;
        rgnBBox:        Rect;
            {optional region definition data}
    end;
```

The rgnSize field contains the size of the Region variable and the rgnBBox field is a rectangle that completely encloses the region.

RgnHandle

The data type RgnHandle is another implementation of double-indirection and is defined as

```
type RgnHandle = ^RgnPtr;
```

This data type is used by QuickDraw to locate an area of memory under Macintosh's double-indirection method of memory management.

RgnPtr

The data type RgnPtr points to the area of memory that contains the variable-length region. It is defined as

```
type RgnPtr = ^Region;
```

Style

The data type Style is used by QuickDraw to define the set of text faces that may be utilized during text drawing operations. It is defined as

```
type StyleItem = (bold, italic, underline, outline, shadow,
                condense, extend);
    Style = set of StyleItem;
```

QuickDraw Graphics Procedures

This section describes the different procedures that may be used to draw graphics images on the screen. QuickDraw has five classes of graphics operations—Frame, Paint, Erase, Invert, and Fill. Figures A-3 through A-6 illustrate the five different classes.

Figure A-3. *Example of QuickDraw operations Frame and Paint*

Figure A-4. *Example of QuickDraw operation Erase*

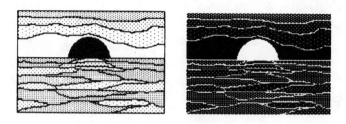

Figure A-5. *Example of QuickDraw operation Invert*

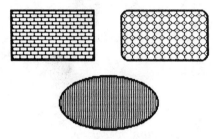

Figure A-6. *Example of QuickDraw operation Fill*

There are 30 QuickDraw Graphics Procedures. They are presented in the following sequence:

EraseArc

EraseOval

ErasePoly

EraseRect

EraseRgn

EraseRoundRect

FillArc

FillOval

FillPoly

FillRect

FillRgn

FillRoundRect

FrameArc

FrameOval

FramePoly

FrameRect

FrameRgn

FrameRoundRect

InvertArc

InvertOval

InvertPoly

InvertRect

InvertRgn

InvertRoundRect

PaintArc

PaintOval

PaintPoly

PaintRect

PaintRgn

PaintRoundRect

procedure EraseArc (r:Rect; startAngle, arcAngle:integer);

Using the current grafPort's background pattern in patCopy mode, EraseArc paints a wedge of the oval just inside the rectangle specified by arc. StartAngle and arcAngle are used in the same manner as in FrameArc. The pen's location is not changed.

procedure EraseOval (r:Rect);

EraseOval forms the specified oval with the current grafPort's background pattern in patCopy mode. The pen's location is not changed.

procedure ErasePoly (poly:PolyHandle);

Using the current grafPort's background pattern in patCopy mode, ErasePoly paints the polygon defined by poly. The pen's location is not changed.

procedure EraseRect (r:Rect);

EraseRect forms the specified rectangle with the current grafPort's background pattern in patCopy mode. The pen's location is not changed.

procedure EraseRgn (rgn:RgnHandle);

Using the current grafPort's background pattern in patCopy mode, the EraseRgn procedure paints the region pointed to by rgn. The pen's location is not changed.

procedure EraseRoundRect (r:Rect; ovalWidth, ovalHeight:integer);

Similar to EraseRect, EraseRoundRect forms the specified round-cornered rectangle with the current grafPort background pattern patCopy mode. The pen's location is not changed.

procedure FillArc (r:Rect; startAngle, arcAngle:integer; pat:Pattern);

Using the pattern specified by pat, FillArc fills the wedge of the oval just inside the rectangle specified by r. StartAngle and arcAngle are used as in FrameArc. The pen's location is not changed.

procedure FillOval (r:Rect; pat:Pattern);

FillOval fills the oval formed just inside the rectangle specified by r with the pattern specified with pat in patCopy mode. The pen's location is not changed.

procedure FillPoly (poly:PolyHandle; pat:Pattern);

Using the pattern specified by pat in patCopy mode, FillPoly paints the polygon pointed to by poly. The pen's location is not changed.

procedure FillRect (r:Rect; pat:Pattern);

FillRect fills the rectangle specified by r with the pattern specified with pat in patCopy mode. The pen's location is not changed.

procedure FillRgn (rgn:RgnHandle; pat:Pattern);

Using the pattern specified by pat, FillRgn fills the region pointed to by rgn. The pen's location is not changed.

procedure FillRoundRect (r:Rect; ovalWidth, ovalHeight:integer; pat:Pattern);

Similar to FillRect, FillRoundRect fills the rectangle specified by r with the pattern specified by pat in patCopy mode. The pen's location is not changed.

procedure FrameArc (r:Rect; startAngle, arcAngle:integer);

Using the current pen pattern, mode, and size, FrameArc draws the arc of the oval that fits inside the rectangle specified by r. StartAngle indicates the angle from which the arc will begin, and arcAngle defines the actual angle of arc that will be drawn. Angles may be positive or negative, with a positive angle indicating the clockwise direction and a negative angle indicating the counterclockwise direction. Figure A-7 indicates the major quadrants with reference to a clock. The arc will be as wide as the pen width and as tall as the pen height. It is drawn with the current pen pattern, according to the pen mode. The pen's location is not changed.

As illustrated in Figure A-8, angles are measured relative to the enclosing rectangle. A line passing through the upper right corner of the rectangle is measured at an angle of 45 degrees, whether or not the enclosing rectangle is square.

procedure FrameOval (r:Rect);

FrameOval forms the outline of an oval that just fits inside the specified rectangle. The outline is as wide as the pen width and as

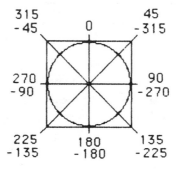

Figure A-7. Major arc quadrants

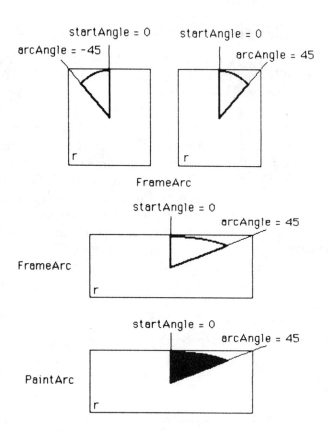

Figure A-8. *Angles measured relative to enclosing rectangles*

tall as the pen height. It is drawn with the current pen pattern, using the pattern transfer mode specified by pnMode. The pen location is not changed by the procedure.

procedure FramePoly (poly:PolyHandle);

Using the current grafPort's pen pattern, mode, and size, Frame-Poly "plays back" the line-drawing routine calls that define the given polygon pointed to by poly. The lines will be as wide as the pen width and as tall as the pen height. Because the pen hangs below and to the right of the pen location, the polygon will extend beyond the right and lower edges of the rectangle in the polyBBox field by the pen width and the pen height, respectively.

If a polygon is open, the line-drawing routines pointed to by poly are added to the outline of the polygon being formed. If a region is open, the outline of the polygon is added mathematically to the region's boundary.

procedure FrameRect (r:Rect);

FrameRect draws the outline of a rectangle using the current pen pattern, mode, and size. The outline will appear just inside the specified rectangle and is as wide as the pen width and as tall as the pen height. It is drawn with the pen pattern according to the pattern transfer mode. The pen location is not changed. If a region is open and being formed, the outline of the new rectangle is added mathematically to the region's boundary.

procedure FrameRgn (rgn:RgnHandle);

Using the current grafPort's pen pattern, mode, and size, Frame-Rgn draws a hollow outline just inside the region pointed to by rgn. The outline will be as wide as the pen width and as tall as the pen height. The pen's location is not changed.

If a region is currently open, the outline of the region pointed to by rgn is added mathematically to the open region's boundary.

procedure FrameRoundRect (r:Rect; ovalWidth, ovalHeight:integer);

As illustrated in Figure A-9, FrameRoundRect draws the outline of a round-cornered rectangle using the current pen pattern, mode, and size. The outline will appear just inside the specified rectangle and is as wide as the pen width and as tall as the pen height. The ovalWidth and ovalHeight are used to size the ovals that form the rounded corners of the rectangle, as shown in Figure A-9. It is drawn with the pen pattern, according to the pattern transfer mode. The pen location is not changed. If a region is open and being formed, the outline of the new round-cornered rectangle is added mathematically to the region's boundary.

procedure InvertArc (r:Rect; startAngle, arcAngle:integer);

InvertArc inverts the pixels enclosed by the wedge of the oval just inside the rectangle specified by r. StartAngle and arcAngle are

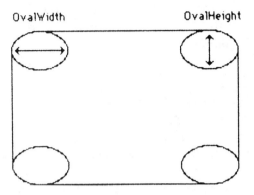

Figure A-9. *A round-cornered rectangle drawn by FrameRoundRect*

used in the same manner as in FrameArc. The pen's location is not changed.

procedure InvertOval (r:Rect);

InvertOval inverts the pixels enclosed by the oval just inside the rectangle specified by r. Each white pixel becomes black and each black pixel becomes white. The pen's location is not changed.

procedure InvertPoly (poly:PolyHandle);

Like InvertRect, InvertPoly inverts the pixels enclosed by the polygon pointed to by poly. Every white pixel becomes black and every black pixel becomes white. The pen's location is not changed.

procedure InvertRect (r:Rect);

InvertRect inverts the pixels enclosed by the rectangle specified by r. Each white pixel becomes black and each black pixel becomes white. The pen's location is not changed.

procedure InvertRgn (rgn:RgnHandle);

Like InvertRect, InvertRgn inverts the pixels enclosed by the region pointed to by rgn. Every white pixel becomes black and every black pixel becomes white. The pen's location is not changed.

procedure InvertRoundRect (r:Rect; ovalWidth, ovalHeight:integer);

Similar to InvertRect, InvertRoundRect inverts the pixels enclosed by the round-cornered rectangle specified by r. Each white pixel becomes black and each black pixel becomes white. The pen's location is not changed.

procedure PaintArc (r:Rect; startAngle, arcAngle:integer);

Using the current grafPort's pen pattern and mode, paintArc paints a wedge of the oval that fits just inside the rectangle specified by r. StartAngle and arcAngle define the arc of the wedge as in FrameArc. The pen's location is not changed.

procedure PaintOval (r:Rect);

Like PaintRect, PaintOval forms an oval just inside the rectangle specified by r. It is drawn with the current pen pattern, using the pattern transfer mode specified by pnMode. The pen location is not changed by the procedure.

procedure PaintPoly (poly:PolyHandle);

Using the current grafPort's pen pattern and pen mode, PaintPoly paints the polygon pointed to by poly. The pen's location is not changed.

procedure PaintRect (r:Rect);

PaintRect draws the specified rectangle filled with the current pen pattern according to the current pen pattern transfer mode. The pen's location is not changed.

procedure PaintRgn (rgn:RgnHandle);

Using the current grafPort's pen pattern and pen mode, PaintRgn paints the region pointed to by rgn. The region is filled with the pen pattern according to the pen mode specified by the current grafPort. The pen's location is not changed.

procedure PaintRoundRect (r:Rect; ovalWidth, ovalHeight:integer);

PaintRoundRect draws the specified round-cornered rectangle filled with the current pen pattern according to the current pen pattern transfer mode. The pen's location is not changed.

Mathematical Systems and Concepts

This appendix presents concepts of Boolean mathematics and describes decimal, binary, and hexadecimal numbering systems.

Concepts of Boolean Mathematics

Boolean logic is a system of mathematical logic first proposed by George Boole in 1857. At that time, mathematicians were excited by the prospect of formulating an entire system of symbolic logic, something hitherto unaccomplished. It was not until the invention of electronic computers, however, that Boolean logic had any practical application outside of mathematics. Now Boolean logic is used to design the electronic circuits that make up a computer. It is thus an integral part of almost all programming languages.

Boolean algebra, like conventional algebra, makes statements that have operators (such as the plus sign for addition or the minus sign for subtraction) and operands (the quantities operated on by the operators). Unlike everyday algebraic equations such as $5 + 7 = 12$, Boolean algebraic expressions may have one of two values—True or False. Boolean operands also take the value of either True or False. The four common logical, or Boolean, operators are NOT, AND, inclusive OR (called OR), and exclusive OR (known as XOR).

NOT

The NOT, or negation operator, performs the same function in Boolean algebra as the word "not" does in the English language. If an element P has the value of True, then NOT P has the value of False. Similarly, NOT False is equivalent to True. The standard format for displaying the results of a Boolean operator on an element or between two elements is the *truth table*. Here is the truth table for NOT:

P	NOT P
T	F
F	T

AND

The AND operator corresponds to the conjunction of two operands. For example, for the expression P AND Q to yield True, *both* P and Q must be True; otherwise, the result will be False. The truth table for AND is as follows:

P	Q	P AND Q
T	T	T
T	F	F
F	T	F
F	F	F

OR

The OR operator corresponds to a disjunction. When *either* operand is True, the entire expression yields True. The truth table for the OR operation is

P	Q	P OR Q
T	T	T
T	F	T
F	T	T
F	F	F

XOR

The XOR operator will yield True only if either operand, but *not both*, is True. XOR's truth table is

P	Q	P XOR Q
T	T	F
T	F	T
F	T	T
F	F	F

Boolean Logic in Programming Languages

All programming languages provide for the use of Boolean operators. Pascal even provides a special data type, Boolean, to handle a variable used in these logical operations. To understand how these variables operate in a program, be advised that an operand can represent one of two binary values. Thus, it is possible to equate the operand with a binary digit, either 1 or 0. By convention, the value of True is equal to 1 (sometimes −1 or NOT 0 in other languages) and the value of False is equal to 0. A series of binary digits, called *bits* for short, may be operated upon element by element. For example:

01101001 NOT
_____
10010110

In the above example, the NOT operator, acting on the series of binary digits 01101001, has as its result the negation of the operand. In NOT, each bit that has the value of 0 is translated into a bit that has the value of 1. Likewise, a value of 1 is converted into a value of 0.

As an example of the Boolean AND operation, look at the following example:

```
01101001
11100011 AND
```
```
01100001
```

The AND operator produces a 1 as a result only if both bits being ANDed are 1's. Otherwise, a 0 is produced. Remember this from the truth table at the beginning of the appendix, where the conjunction of two operands was True only when both were themselves True. All other combinations produced False.

An example of the OR logical operation is

```
01101001
11100011 OR
```
```
11101011
```

The OR operator generates a 1 if there is a 1 in either of the two bits being compared. A 0 is returned only if both bits being compared are 0. Again, think back to the truth table for the OR operation, where the result was True when either (or both) of the operands were True and False only when both operands were False.

Unlike the standard OR operation, the XOR operation takes a "one or the other, but not both" approach to making its decisions. Look at this example:

```
01101001
11100011 XOR
```
```
10001010
```

The XOR operation produces a 1 if either of the bits being compared contains a 1. In any other case, a 0 is returned as the answer.

Although the techniques borrowed from Boolean logic are important to a programming language for controlling program flow, the Macintosh uses Boolean techniques for transferring graphics images as well as for their more conventional role of directing program flow.

Numbering Systems

Many Macintosh applications require the use of a diverse set of graphics techniques to control the appearance of the Macintosh screen. The use of these techniques depends heavily on a knowledge of numbering systems other than the standard decimal system used almost everywhere. The following section explains the different numbering systems used by computers and illustrates their application to programming the Macintosh.

Decimal

The numbering system we use on a day-to-day basis is known as the *decimal system*. It has a set of ten digits labeled 0 through 9. Each digit position in a decimal number represents a power of ten, as illustrated below:

Digit Position

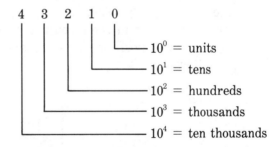

so that the decimal number 62,023 is equal to

$$
\begin{array}{rcl}
6 \times 10,000 & = & 60,000 \\
2 \times 1,000 & = & 2,000 \\
0 \times 100 & = & 0 \\
2 \times 10 & = & 20 \\
3 \times 1 & = & 3 \\
\hline
& & 62,023
\end{array}
$$

Each decimal position is multiplied by the power of ten represented by that position. These values are then added together to form the total. The decimal system is said to be *base 10*. That is, there are a total of ten elements composing the set of possible digits.

Other numbering systems use numbers other than 10 as their base. The *binary* system, which we just saw in the previous section on Boolean logic, is also called *base 2* because only the digits 0 and 1 are utilized. *Octal*, also called *base 8*, uses the digits 0, 1, 2, 3, 4, 5, 6, and 7. *Hexadecimal*, also referred to as *base 16*, uses the digits 0 through 9 and then the letters A, B, C, D, E, and F to represent the decimal values 10 through 15.

Binary

The decimal system is not a very useful system for computers because it is difficult for a computer to distinguish among ten different digits. Binary was chosen as the numbering system for computers because it is very easy to represent the binary digits in the electronic circuitry that make up a computer. Electronically, the binary digits 0 and 1 can be represented by a switch that is either on or off. You can liken this to a light switch. When on, the light is incandescent. This corresponds to a True state. When flipped off, the light goes out and the circuit is in a False state.

Each digit position in the binary system represents a power of 2 as follows:

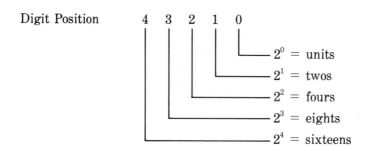

The binary number 10110 is therefore equal to:

$$
\begin{array}{rcl}
1 \times 16 & = & 16 \\
0 \times 8 & = & 0 \\
1 \times 4 & = & 4 \\
1 \times 2 & = & 2 \\
0 \times 1 & = & 0 \\
\hline
\end{array}
$$

22 in decimal

The previous example demonstrates how to convert from the

binary number system to the decimal number system. It is very easy for a computer to store the number 19 as a binary number. Imagine the computer's memory as a row of five switches. The first switch is on, indicating a value of sixteen. The second switch is off, indicating a value of 0, and so on for each switch. Converting from decimal to binary is just as simple as converting from binary to decimal. The procedure consists of a series of repeated steps. Each time the procedure is repeated, it returns the next higher digit position.

In order to convert decimal numbers into binary numbers, follow these steps:

1. Divide the decimal number by 2.

2. If there is a remainder from the division, write down the number 1; otherwise, write down the number 0.

3. Discard the remainder and use the quotient obtained earlier as the dividend in the next division.

4. Repeat steps 1 through 3 until you obtain 1 as the quotient. This last 1 becomes the last binary digit in the number.

Converting the decimal number 22 into binary is shown in the following example:

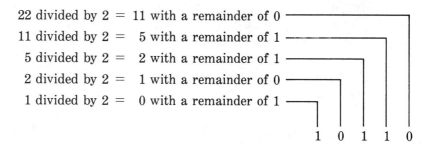

22 divided by 2 = 11 with a remainder of 0
11 divided by 2 = 5 with a remainder of 1
 5 divided by 2 = 2 with a remainder of 1
 2 divided by 2 = 1 with a remainder of 0
 1 divided by 2 = 0 with a remainder of 1

1   0   1   1   0

Thus, the number 22 in decimal is 10110 in binary. The best way to understand these conversions is to practice them.

Hexadecimal

As with decimal numbers, binary numbers may be added, subtracted, divided, and multiplied. However, for the purposes of this book, it is not necessary to understand the basic operations of binary arithmetic. What is important to know is how to use hexadecimal notation. Because it is extremely easy to make a mistake when dealing with long strings of binary numbers, the practice of converting binary numbers into hexadecimal numbers for easier manipulation has developed. Hexadecimal is a numbering system that uses the base 16 (which is a power of 2). Each digit position of a hexadecimal number represents powers of sixteen as follows:

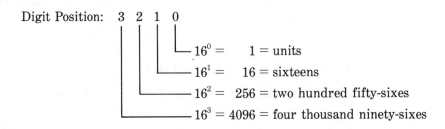

Digit Position: 3 2 1 0

$16^0 =$ 1 = units
$16^1 =$ 16 = sixteens
$16^2 =$ 256 = two hundred fifty-sixes
$16^3 =$ 4096 = four thousand ninety-sixes

The hexadecimal system uses the sixteen digits labeled 0 though 9 plus the alphabetic characters A through F to represent the values 10 through 15, respectively. The use of the hexadecimal number system may seem extremely clumsy until the organization of the computer's memory is taken into consideration. As previously mentioned, the computer's memory is organized as an array of switches, with each switch representing one bit. This array of switches is organized further into groups of eight bits, each group commonly known as a *byte*. Because 16 is the fourth power of two, conversion from a binary number to a hexadecimal number is both simple and direct. And because any hexadecimal number can be represented by four bits, a byte can be represented by two hexadecimal numbers. For example:

```
      0100 binary  =   4 hexadecimal  =   4 decimal
      1111 binary  =   F hexadecimal  =  15 decimal
  01001111 binary  =  4F hexadecimal  =  79 decimal
```

This simple conversion makes it easy to code long binary strings in a program without worrying about binary-to-decimal conversion. This conversion is extremely important in a graphics computer like the Macintosh because the graphics images that appear on the Macintosh screen are held in memory as a series of bits called *bit images.*

As you read in the beginning of this book, the Macintosh's screen is made up of a grid of dots called pixels. Each pixel is represented somewhere in the Macintosh's memory as a single bit. You can imagine what it would be like trying to write a binary string of digits with enough bits in it to describe even a simple picture on the screen. It would be extremely easy to make a mistake. Using hexadecimal numbers reduces the chance for error and is much quicker to write and test.

Hexadecimal to Decimal Conversion Chart

Column = first nibble (4 bytes) of byte.
Row   = second nibble (4 bytes) of byte.

	0	1	2	3	4	5	6	7	8	9	A	B	C	D	E	F
0	0	1	2	3	4	5	6	7	8	9	10	11	12	13	14	15
1	16	17	18	19	20	21	22	23	24	25	26	27	28	29	30	31
2	32	33	34	35	36	37	38	39	40	41	42	43	44	45	46	47
3	48	49	50	51	52	53	54	55	56	57	58	59	60	61	62	63
4	64	65	66	67	68	69	70	71	72	73	74	75	76	77	78	79
5	80	81	82	83	84	85	86	87	88	89	90	91	92	93	94	95
6	96	97	98	99	100	101	102	103	104	105	106	107	108	109	110	111
7	112	113	114	115	116	117	118	119	120	121	122	123	124	125	126	127
8	128	129	130	131	132	133	134	135	136	137	138	139	140	141	142	143
9	144	145	146	147	148	149	150	151	152	153	154	155	156	157	158	159
A	160	161	162	163	164	165	166	167	168	169	170	171	172	173	174	175
B	176	177	178	179	180	181	182	183	184	185	186	187	188	189	190	191
C	192	193	194	195	196	197	198	199	200	201	202	203	204	205	206	207
D	208	209	210	211	212	213	214	215	216	217	218	219	220	221	222	223
E	224	225	226	227	228	229	230	231	232	233	234	235	236	237	238	239
F	240	241	242	243	244	245	246	247	248	249	250	251	252	253	254	255

Macintosh Trap Locations

Macintosh Trap Locations Listed by Trap Address		Macintosh Trap Locations Listed by Trap Name	
Trap Name	**Address**	**Trap Name**	**Address**
Open	A000	AddDrive	A04E
Close	A001	AddPt	A87E
Read	A002	AddReference	A9AC
Write	A003	AddResMenu	A94D

Macintosh Trap Locations
Listed by
Trap Address

Macintosh Trap Locations
Listed by
Trap Name

Trap Name	Address	Trap Name	Address
Control	A004	AddResource	A9AB
Status	A005	Alert	A985
KillIO	A006	AngleFromSlope	A8C4
GetVolInfo	A007	AppendMenu	A933
FileCreate	A008	BackColor	A863
FileDelete	A009	BackPat	A87C
OpenRf	A00A	BeginUpdate	A922
Rename	A00B	BitAnd	A858
GetFileInfo	A00C	BitClr	A85F
SetFileInfo	A00D	BitNot	A85A
UnmountVol	A00E	BitOr	A85B
MountVol	A00F	BitSet	A85E
FileAllocate	A010	BitShift	A85C
GetEOF	A011	BitTst	A85D
SetEOF	A012	BitXor	A859
FlushVol	A013	BlockMove	A02E
GetVol	A014	BringToFront	A920
SetVol	A015	Button	A974
FInitQueue	A016	CalcMenuSize	A948
Eject	A017	CalcVis	A909
GetFPos	A018	CalcVisBehind	A90A
InitZone	A019	CautionAlert	A988
GetZone	A01A	Chain	A9F3
SetZone	A01B	ChangedResData	A9AA
FreeMem	A01C	CharWidth	A88D
MaxMem	A01D	CheckItem	A945
NewPtr	A01E	CheckUpdate	A911
DisposePtr	A01F	ClearMenuBar	A934
SetPtrSize	A020	ClipAbove	A90B
GetPtrSize	A021	ClipRect	A87B
NWHandle	A022	Close	A001
DsposeHandle	A023	CloseDeskAcc	A9B7
SetHandleSize	A024	CloseDialog	A982
GetHandleSize	A025	ClosePicture	A8F4
HandleZone	A026	ClosePoly	A8CC
ReAllocHandle	A027	ClosePort	A87D
RecoverHandle	A028	CloseResFile	A99A
HLock	A029	CloseRgn	A8DB
HUnlock	A02A	CloseWindow	A92D
EmptyHandle	A02B	CmpString	A03C
InitApplZone	A02C	ColorBit	A864
SetApplLimit	A02D	CompactMem	A04C
BlockMove	A02E	Control	A004

Macintosh Trap Locations
Listed by
Trap Address

Macintosh Trap Locations
Listed by
Trap Name

Trap Name	Address	Trap Name	Address
PostEvent	A02F	CopyBits	A8EC
OSEventAvail	A030	CopyRgn	A8DC
GetOSEvent	A031	CouldAlert	A989
FlushEvents	A032	CouldDialog	A979
VInstall	A033	CountMItems	A950
VRemove	A034	CountResources	A99C
OffLine	A035	CountTypes	A99E
MoreMasters	A036	CreateResFile	A9B1
ReadParam	A037	CurResFile	A994
WrtiteParam	A038	DeQueue	A96E
ReadDateTime	A039	Delay	A03B
SetDateTime	A03A	DeleteMenu	A936
Delay	A03B	DeltaPoint	A94F
CmpString	A03C	DetatchResource	A992
DrvrInstall	A03D	DialogSelect	A980
DrvrRemove	A03E	DiffRgn	A8E6
InitUtil	A03F	DisableItem	A93A
ResrvMem	A040	DisposeControl	A955
SetFilLock	A041	DisposeDialog	A983
RstFilLock	A042	DisposeMenu	A932
SetFilType	A043	DisposePtr	A01F
SetFPos	A044	DisposeRgn	A8D9
FlushFil	A045	DisposeWindow	A914
GetTrapAddress	A046	DragControl	A967
SetTrapAddress	A047	DragGrayRgn	A905
PtrZone	A048	DragTheRgn	A926
HHPurge	A049	DragWindow	A925
HNoPurge	A04A	DrawChar	A883
SetGrowZone	A04B	DrawControls	A969
CompactMem	A04C	DrawDialog	A981
PurgeMem	A04D	DrawGrowIcon	A904
AddDrive	A04E	DrawMenuBar	A937
InstallRDrivers	A04F	DrawNew	A90F
InitCursor	A850	DrawPicture	A8F6
SetCursor	A851	DrawString	A884
HideCursor	A852	DrawText	A885
ShowCursor	A853	DrvrInstall	A03D
UprString	A854	DrvrRemove	A03E
ShieldCursor	A855	DisposeHandle	A023
ObscureCursor	A856	Eject	A017
SetApplBase	A857	EmptyHandle	A02B
BitAnd	A858	EmptyRect	A8AE
BitXor	A859	EmptyRgn	A8E2

Macintosh Trap Locations
Listed by
Trap Address

Macintosh Trap Locations
Listed by
Trap Name

Trap Name	Address	Trap Name	Address
BitNot	A85A	EnQueue	A96F
BitOr	A85B	EnableItem	A939
BitShift	A85C	EndUpdate	A923
BitTst	A85D	EqualPt	A881
BitSet	A85E	EqualRect	A8A6
BitClr	A85F	EqualRgn	A8E3
Random	A861	EraseArc	A8C0
ForeColor	A862	EraseOval	A8B9
BackColor	A863	ErasePoly	A8C8
ColorBit	A864	EraseRect	A8A3
GetPixel	A865	EraseRgn	A8D4
StuffHex	A866	EraseRoundRect	A8B2
LongMul	A867	ErrorSound	A98C
FixMul	A868	EventAvail	A971
FixRatio	A869	ExitToShell	A9F4
HiWord	A86A	FInitQueue	A016
LoWord	A86B	FMSwapFont	A901
FixRound	A86C	FileAllocate	A010
InitPort	A86D	FileCreate	A008
InitGraf	A86E	FileDelete	A009
OpenPort	A86F	FillArc	A8C2
LocalToGlobal	A870	FillOval	A8BB
GlobalToLocal	A871	FillPoly	A8CA
GrafDevice	A872	FillRect	A8A5
SetPort	A873	FillRgn	A8D6
GetPort	A874	FillRoundRect	A8B4
SetPortBits	A875	FindControl	A96C
PortSize	A876	FindWindow	A92C
MovePortTo	A877	FixMul	A868
SetOrigin	A878	FixRatio	A869
SetClip	A879	FixRound	A86C
GetClip	A87A	FlashMenuBar	A94C
ClipRect	A87B	FlushEvents	A032
BackPat	A87C	FlushFil	A045
ClosePort	A87D	FlushVol	A013
AddPt	A87E	ForeColor	A862
SubPt	A87F	FrameArc	A8BE
SetPt	A880	FrameOval	A8B7
EqualPt	A881	FramePoly	A8C6
StdText	A882	FrameRect	A8A1
DrawChar	A883	FrameRgn	A8D2
DrawString	A884	FrameRoundRect	A8B0
DrawText	A885	FreeAlert	A98A

Macintosh Trap Locations
Listed by
Trap Address

Macintosh Trap Locations
Listed by
Trap Name

Trap Name	Address	Trap Name	Address
TextWidth	A886	FreeDialog	A97A
TextFont	A887	FreeMem	A01C
TextFace	A888	FrontWindow	A924
TextMode	A889	GetAppParms	A9F5
TextSize	A88A	GetCRefCon	A95A
GetFontInfo	A88B	GetCTitle	A95E
StringWidth	A88C	GetClip	A87A
CharWidth	A88D	GetCtlAction	A96A
SpaceExtra	A88E	GetCtlMax	A962
StdLine	A890	GetCtlMin	A961
LineTo	A891	GetCtlValue	A960
Line	A892	GetCursor	A9B9
MoveTo	A893	GetDItem	A98D
Move	A894	GetEOF	A011
HidePen	A896	GetFNum	A900
ShowPen	A897	GetFPos	A018
GetPenState	A898	GetFileInfo	A00C
SetPenState	A899	GetFontInfo	A88B
GetPen	A89A	GetFontName	A8FF
PenSize	A89B	GetHandleSize	A025
PenMode	A89C	GetIText	A990
PenPat	A89D	GetIcon	A9BB
PenNormal	A89E	GetIndResource	A99D
StdRect	A8A0	GetIndType	A99F
FrameRect	A8A1	GetItem	A946
PaintRect	A8A2	GetItemIcon	A93F
EraseRect	A8A3	GetItemMark	A943
InvertRect	A8A4	GetItemStyle	A941
FillRect	A8A5	GetKeys	A976
EqualRect	A8A6	GetMHandle	A949
SetRect	A8A7	GetMenu	A9BF
OffsetRect	A8A8	GetMenuBar	A93B
InsetRect	A8A9	GetMouse	A972
SectRect	A8AA	GetNamedResourc	A9A1
UnionRect	A8AB	GetNewControl	A9BE
Pt2Rect	A8AC	GetNewDialog	A97C
PtInRect	A8AD	GetNewMBar	A9C0
EmptyRect	A8AE	GetNewWindow	A9BD
StdRRect	A8AF	GetNextEvent	A970
FrameRoundRect	A8B0	GetOSEvent	A031
PaintRoundRect	A8B1	GetPattern	A9B8
EraseRoundRect	A8B2	GetPen	A89A
InvertRoundRect	A8B3	GetPenState	A898

Macintosh Trap Locations
Listed by
Trap Address

Macintosh Trap Locations
Listed by
Trap Name

Trap Name	Address	Trap Name	Address
FillRoundRect	A8B4	GetPicture	A9BC
StdOval	A8B6	GetPixel	A865
FrameOval	A8B7	GetPort	A874
PaintOval	A8B8	GetPtrSize	A021
EraseOval	A8B9	GetResAttrs	A9A6
InvertOval	A8BA	GetResFileAttrs	A9F6
FillOval	A8BB	GetResInfo	A9A8
SlopeFromAngle	A8BC	GetResource	A9A0
StdArc	A8BD	GetScrap	A9FD
FrameArc	A8BE	GetString	A9BA
PaintArc	A8BF	GetTrapAddress	A046
EraseArc	A8C0	GetVol	A014
InvertArc	A8C1	GetVolInfo	A007
FillArc	A8C2	GetWMgrPort	A910
PtToAngle	A8C3	GetWRefCon	A917
AngleFromSlope	A8C4	GetWTitle	A919
StdPoly	A8C5	GetWindowPic	A92F
FramePoly	A8C6	GetZone	A01A
PaintPoly	A8C7	GlobalToLocal	A871
ErasePoly	A8C8	GrafDevice	A872
InvertPoly	A8C9	GrowWindow	A92B
FillPoly	A8CA	HHPurge	A049
OpenPoly	A8CB	HLock	A029
ClosePoly	A8CC	HNoPurge	A04A
KillPoly	A8CD	HUnlock	A02A
OffsetPoly	A8CE	HandAndHand	A9E4
PackBits	A8CF	HandToHand	A9E1
UnPackBits	A8D0	HandleZone	A026
StdRgn	A8D1	HiWord	A86A
FrameRgn	A8D2	HideControl	A958
PaintRgn	A8D3	HideCursor	A852
EraseRgn	A8D4	HidePen	A896
InvertRgn	A8D5	HideWindow	A916
FillRgn	A8D6	HiliteControl	A95D
NewRgn	A8D8	HiliteMenu	A938
DisposeRgn	A8D9	HiliteWindow	A91C
OpenRgn	A8DA	HomeResFile	A9A4
CloseRgn	A8DB	InfoScrap	A9F9
CopyRgn	A8DC	InitApplZone	A02C
SetEmptyRgn	A8DD	InitCursor	A850
SetRectRgn	A8DE	InitDialogs	A97B
RectRgn	A8DF	InitFonts	A8FE
OffsetRgn	A8E0	InitGraf	A86E

Macintosh Trap Locations
Listed by
Trap Address

Macintosh Trap Locations
Listed by
Trap Name

Trap Name	Address	Trap Name	Address
InsetRgn	A8E1	InitMath	A9E6
EmptyRgn	A8E2	InitMenus	A930
EqualRgn	A8E3	InitPack	A9E5
SectRgn	A8E4	InitPort	A86D
UnionRgn	A8E5	InitResources	A995
DiffRgn	A8E6	InitUtil	A03F
XorRgn	A8E7	InitWindows	A912
PtInRgn	A8E8	InitZone	A019
RectInRgn	A8E9	InsertMenu	A935
SetStdProcs	A8EA	InsertResMenu	A951
StdBits	A8EB	InsetRect	A8A9
CopyBits	A8EC	InsetRgn	A8E1
StdTxMeasure	A8ED	InstallRDrivers	A04F
StdGetPic	A8EE	InvalRect	A928
ScrollRect	A8EF	InvalRgn	A927
StdPutPic	A8F0	InvertArc	A8C1
StdComment	A8F1	InvertOval	A8BA
PicComment	A8F2	InvertPoly	A8C9
OpenPicture	A8F3	InvertRect	A8A4
ClosePicture	A8F4	InvertRgn	A8D5
KillPicture	A8F5	InvertRoundRect	A8B3
DrawPicture	A8F6	IsDialogEvent	A97F
ScalePt	A8F8	KillControls	A956
MapPt	A8F9	KillIO	A006
MapRect	A8FA	KillPicture	A8F5
MapRgn	A8FB	KillPoly	A8CD
MapPoly	A8FC	Launch	A9F2
InitFonts	A8FE	Line	A892
GetFontName	A8FF	LineTo	A891
GetFNum	A900	LoWord	A86B
FMSwapFont	A901	LoadResource	A9A2
RealFont	A902	LoadScrap	A9FB
SetFontLock	A903	LoadSeg	A9F0
DrawGrowIcon	A904	LocalToGlobal	A870
DragGrayRgn	A905	LongMul	A867
NewString	A906	MapPoly	A8FC
SetString	A907	MapPt	A8F9
ShowHide	A908	MapRect	A8FA
CalcVis	A909	MapRgn	A8FB
CalcVisBehind	A90A	MaxMem	A01D
ClipAbove	A90B	MenuKey	A93E
PaintOne	A90C	MenuSelect	A93D
PaintBehind	A90D	ModalDialog	A991

Macintosh Trap Locations
Listed by
Trap Address

Macintosh Trap Locations
Listed by
Trap Name

Trap Name	Address	Trap Name	Address
SaveOld	A90E	MoreMasters	A036
DrawNew	A90F	MountVol	A00F
GetWMgrPort	A910	Move	A894
CheckUpdate	A911	MoveControl	A959
InitWindows	A912	MovePortTo	A877
NewWindow	A913	MoveTo	A893
DisposeWindow	A914	MoveWindow	A91B
ShowWindow	A915	Munger	A9E0
HideWindow	A916	NWHandle	A022
GetWRefCon	A917	NewControl	A954
SetWRefCon	A918	NewDialog	A97D
GetWTitle	A919	NewMenu	A931
SetWTitle	A91A	NewPtr	A01E
MoveWindow	A91B	NewRgn	A8D8
HiliteWindow	A91C	NewString	A906
SizeWindow	A91D	NewWindow	A913
TrackGoAway	A91E	NoteAlert	A987
SelectWindow	A91F	OSEventAvail	A030
BringToFront	A920	ObscureCursor	A856
SendBehind	A921	OffLine	A035
BeginUpdate	A922	OffsetPoly	A8CE
EndUpdate	A923	OffsetRect	A8A8
FrontWindow	A924	OffsetRgn	A8E0
DragWindow	A925	Open	A000
DragTheRgn	A926	OpenDeskAcc	A9B6
InvalRgn	A927	OpenPicture	A8F3
InvalRect	A928	OpenPoly	A8CB
ValidRgn	A929	OpenPort	A86F
ValidRect	A92A	OpenResFile	A997
GrowWindow	A92B	OpenRf	A00A
FindWindow	A92C	OpenRgn	A8DA
CloseWindow	A92D	Pack0	A9E7
SetWindowPic	A92E	Pack1	A9E8
GetWindowPic	A92F	Pack2	A9E9
InitMenus	A930	Pack3	A9EA
NewMenu	A931	Pack4	A9EB
DisposeMenu	A932	Pack5	A9EC
AppendMenu	A933	Pack6	A9ED
ClearMenuBar	A934	Pack7	A9EE
InsertMenu	A935	PackBits	A8CF
DeleteMenu	A936	PaintArc	A8BF
DrawMenuBar	A937	PaintBehind	A90D
HiliteMenu	A938	PaintOne	A90C

Macintosh Trap Locations
Listed by
Trap Address

Macintosh Trap Locations
Listed by
Trap Name

Trap Name	Address	Trap Name	Address
EnableItem	A939	PaintOval	A8B8
DisableItem	A93A	PaintPoly	A8C7
GetMenuBar	A93B	PaintRect	A8A2
SetMenuBar	A93C	PaintRgn	A8D3
MenuSelect	A93D	PaintRoundRect	A8B1
MenuKey	A93E	ParamText	A98B
GetItemIcon	A93F	PenMode	A89C
SetItemIcon	A940	PenNormal	A89E
GetItemStyle	A941	PenPat	A89D
SetItemStyle	A942	PenSize	A89B
GetItemMark	A943	PicComment	A8F2
SetItemMark	A944	PinRect	A94E
CheckItem	A945	PlotIcon	A94B
GetItem	A946	PortSize	A876
SetItem	A947	PostEvent	A02F
CalcMenuSize	A948	Pt2Rect	A8AC
GetMHandle	A949	PtInRect	A8AD
SetMenuFlash	A94A	PtInRgn	A8E8
PlotIcon	A94B	PtToAngle	A8C3
FlashMenuBar	A94C	PtrAndHand	A9EF
AddResMenu	A94D	PtrToHand	A9E3
PinRect	A94E	PtrToXHand	A9E2
DeltaPoint	A94F	PtrZone	A048
CountMItems	A950	PurgeMem	A04D
InsertResMenu	A951	PutIcon	A9CA
NewControl	A954	PutScrap	A9FE
DisposeControl	A955	Random	A861
KillControls	A956	ReAllocHandle	A027
ShowControl	A957	Read	A002
HideControl	A958	ReadDateTime	A039
MoveControl	A959	ReadParam	A037
GetCRefCon	A95A	RealFont	A902
SetCRefCon	A95B	RecoverHandle	A028
SizeControl	A95C	RectInRgn	A8E9
HiliteControl	A95D	RectRgn	A8DF
GetCTitle	A95E	ReleaseResource	A9A3
SetCTitle	A95F	Rename	A00B
GetCtlValue	A960	ResError	A9AF
GetCtlMin	A961	ResrvMem	A040
GetCtlMax	A962	RmveReference	A9AE
SetCtlValue	A963	RmveResource	A9AD
SetCtlMin	A964	RsrcZoneInit	A996
SetCtlMax	A965	RstFilLock	A042

Macintosh Trap Locations
Listed by
Trap Address

Macintosh Trap Locations
Listed by
Trap Name

Trap Name	Address	Trap Name	Address
TestControl	A966	SaveOld	A90E
DragControl	A967	ScalePt	A8F8
TrackControl	A968	ScrollRect	A8EF
DrawControls	A969	SectRect	A8AA
GetCtlAction	A96A	SectRgn	A8E4
SetCtlAction	A96B	SelectWindow	A91F
FindControl	A96C	SendBehind	A921
DeQueue	A96E	SetApplBase	A857
EnQueue	A96F	SetApplLimit	A02D
GetNextEvent	A970	SetCRefCon	A95B
EventAvail	A971	SetCTitle	A95F
GetMouse	A972	SetClip	A879
StillDown	A973	SetCtlAction	A96B
Button	A974	SetCtlMax	A965
TickCount	A975	SetCtlMin	A964
GetKeys	A976	SetCtlValue	A963
WaitMouseUp	A977	SetCursor	A851
CouldDialog	A979	SetDItem	A98E
FreeDialog	A97A	SetDateTime	A03A
InitDialogs	A97B	SetEOF	A012
GetNewDialog	A97C	SetEmptyRgn	A8DD
NewDialog	A97D	SetFPos	A044
SetIText	A97E	SetFilLock	A041
IsDialogEvent	A97F	SetFilType	A043
DialogSelect	A980	SetFileInfo	A00D
DrawDialog	A981	SetFontLock	A903
CloseDialog	A982	SetGrowZone	A04B
DisposeDialog	A983	SetHandleSize	A024
Alert	A985	SetIText	A97E
StopAlert	A986	SetIText	A98F
NoteAlert	A987	SetItem	A947
CautionAlert	A988	SetItemIcon	A940
CouldAlert	A989	SetItemMark	A944
FreeAlert	A98A	SetItemStyle	A942
ParamText	A98B	SetMenuBar	A93C
ErrorSound	A98C	SetMenuFlash	A94A
GetDItem	A98D	SetOrigin	A878
SetDItem	A98E	SetPenState	A899
SetIText	A98F	SetPort	A873
GetIText	A990	SetPortBits	A875
ModalDialog	A991	SetPt	A880
DetachResource	A992	SetPtrSize	A020
SetResPurge	A993	SetRect	A8A7

Macintosh Trap Locations
Listed by
Trap Address

Macintosh Trap Locations
Listed by
Trap Name

Trap Name	Address	Trap Name	Address
CurResFile	A994	SetRectRgn	A8DE
InitResources	A995	SetResAttrs	A9A7
RsrcZoneInit	A996	SetResFileAttrs	A9F7
OpenResFile	A997	SetResInfo	A9A9
UseResFile	A998	SetResLoad	A99B
UpdateResFile	A999	SetResPurge	A993
CloseResFile	A99A	SetStdProcs	A8EA
SetResLoad	A99B	SetString	A907
CountResources	A99C	SetTrapAddress	A047
GetIndResource	A99D	SetVol	A015
CountTypes	A99E	SetWRefCon	A918
GetIndType	A99F	SetWTitle	A91A
GetResource	A9A0	SetWindowPic	A92E
GetNamedResourc	A9A1	SetZone	A01B
LoadResource	A9A2	ShieldCursor	A855
ReleaseResource	A9A3	ShowControl	A957
HomeResFile	A9A4	ShowCursor	A853
SizeRsrc	A9A5	ShowHide	A908
GetResAttrs	A9A6	ShowPen	A897
SetResAttrs	A9A7	ShowWindow	A915
GetResInfo	A9A8	SizeControl	A95C
SetResInfo	A9A9	SizeRsrc	A9A5
ChangedResData	A9AA	SizeWindow	A91D
AddResource	A9AB	SlopeFromAngle	A8BC
AddReference	A9AC	SpaceExtra	A88E
RmveResource	A9AD	Status	A005
RmveReference	A9AE	StdArc	A8BD
ResError	A9AF	StdBits	A8EB
WriteResource	A9B0	StdComment	A8F1
CreateResFile	A9B1	StdGetPic	A8EE
SystemEvent	A9B2	StdLine	A890
SystemClick	A9B3	StdOval	A8B6
SystemTask	A9B4	StdPoly	A8C5
SystemMenu	A9B5	StdPutPic	A8F0
OpenDeskAcc	A9B6	StdRRect	A8AF
CloseDeskAcc	A9B7	StdRect	A8A0
GetPattern	A9B8	StdRgn	A8D1
GetCursor	A9B9	StdText	A882
GetString	A9BA	StdTxMeasure	A8ED
GetIcon	A9BB	StillDown	A973
GetPicture	A9BC	StopAlert	A986
GetNewWindow	A9BD	StringWidth	A88C
GetNewControl	A9BE	StuffHex	A866

Macintosh Trap Locations
Listed by
Trap Address

Macintosh Trap Locations
Listed by
Trap Name

Trap Name	Address	Trap Name	Address
GetMenu	A9BF	SubPt	A87F
GetNewMBar	A9C0	SystemBeep	A9C8
UniqueID	A9C1	SystemClick	A9B3
SystemEdit	A9C2	SystemEdit	A9C2
SystemBeep	A9C8	SystemError	A9C9
SystemError	A9C9	SystemEvent	A9B2
PutIcon	A9CA	SystemMenu	A9B5
TEGetText	A9CB	SystemTask	A9B4
TEInit	A9CC	TEActivate	A9D8
TEDispose	A9CD	TECalText	A9D0
TextBox	A9CE	TEClick	A9D4
TESetText	A9CF	TECopy	A9D5
TECalText	A9D0	TECut	A9D6
TESetSelect	A9D1	TEDeactivate	A9D9
TENew	A9D2	TEDelete	A9D7
TEUpdate	A9D3	TEDispose	A9CD
TEClick	A9D4	TEGetText	A9CB
TECopy	A9D5	TEIdle	A9DA
TECut	A9D6	TEInit	A9CC
TEDelete	A9D7	TEInsert	A9DE
TEActivate	A9D8	TEKey	A9DC
TEDeactivate	A9D9	TENew	A9D2
TEIdle	A9DA	TEPaste	A9DB
TEPaste	A9DB	TEScroll	A9DD
TEKey	A9DC	TESetJust	A9DF
TEScroll	A9DD	TESetSelect	A9D1
TEInsert	A9DE	TESetText	A9CF
TESetJust	A9DF	TEUpdate	A9D3
Munger	A9E0	TestControl	A966
HandToHand	A9E1	TextBox	A9CE
PtrToXHand	A9E2	TextFace	A888
PtrToHand	A9E3	TextFont	A887
HandAndHand	A9E4	TextMode	A889
InitPack	A9E5	TextSize	A88A
InitMath	A9E6	TextWidth	A886
Pack0	A9E7	TickCount	A975
Pack1	A9E8	TrackControl	A968
Pack2	A9E9	TrackGoAway	A91E
Pack3	A9EA	UnLoadSeg	A9F1
Pack4	A9EB	UnPackBits	A8D0
Pack5	A9EC	UnionRect	A8AB
Pack6	A9ED	UnionRgn	A8E5
Pack7	A9EE	UniqueID	A9C1

Macintosh Trap Locations
Listed by
Trap Address

Trap Name	Address
PtrAndHand	A9EF
LoadSeg	A9F0
UnLoadSeg	A9F1
Launch	A9F2
Chain	A9F3
ExitToShell	A9F4
GetAppParms	A9F5
GetResFileAttrs	A9F6
SetResFileAttrs	A9F7
InfoScrap	A9F9
UnloadScrap	A9FA
LoadScrap	A9FB
ZeroScrap	A9FC
GetScrap	A9FD
PutScrap	A9FE

Macintosh Trap Locations
Listed by
Trap Name

Trap Name	Address
UnloadScrap	A9FA
UnmountVol	A00E
UpdateResFile	A999
UprString	A854
UseResFile	A998
VInstall	A033
VRemove	A034
ValidRect	A92A
ValidRgn	A929
WaitMouseUp	A977
Write	A003
WriteResource	A9B0
WrtiteParam	A038
XorRgn	A8E7
ZeroScrap	A9FC

G L O S S A R Y

The following glossary contains terms and phrases used in this book. A number of other terms that relate to computers in general and the Macintosh in particular have been added.

Abort: To stop processing.

Access: To get at. Information, both in memory and on disk files, may be accessed through applications programs.

Accessories: Small applications generally available to the user at all times. On the Macintosh, these applications perform such functions as displaying an alarm clock, a calculator, and a puzzle.

Activate Event: An event generated by the Window Manager when a window becomes active.

Active Window: The front-most window on the desktop. The window in which any data typed by a user appears.

Address: The numerical digits (whether in binary, decimal, or hexadecimal) that identify a particular location in memory.

Alert Box: A kind of window containing warnings and cautions displayed by an application when it encounters a problem.

Alert Message: An audible or visible message or warning generated by an application to signal input errors, problems relating to the interpretation of data, or situations threatening the safety of a user's information.

Algorithm: A set of calculating procedures. An algorithm can be thought of as a series of steps designed to solve a problem.

Allocate: To set apart and designate for a purpose. The Macintosh allocates memory for menus, screens, icons, and other internal functions. Various procedures are used within Macintosh Pascal to obtain and free available memory space as needed.

Alphanumeric: Any alphabetic or numeric character produced using the standard keyboard. Alphanumerics do not include special characters.

Applications Window: The window created by an applications program either directly via the Window Manager or indirectly via the Dialog Manager.

Array: A collection of data organized in matrix fashion, all of the same data type. Arrays use subscripts to indicate the location of particular elements in the array.

Ascent: The vertical distance from a font's baseline to its ascent line.

Ascent Line: A horizontal line coincident with the top of the tallest characters in a font.

ASCII: The standard character set used on most microcomputers. ASCII is the acronym for American Standard Code for Information Interchange.

Assembler: A piece of software designed to translate assembly language source code into directly executable machine code.

Assembly Language: A very low-level language that uses macros and simple commands to perform single operations at the machine level. Assembly language is one step higher than actual machine language.

BASIC: The programming language (Beginner's All-Purpose Symbolic Instruction Code) that first used interpreters.

Binary: The base two numbering system, in which numbers are formed exclusively from the digits 0 and 1.

Bit: A common contraction for binary digit. This is the smallest unit of storage within a computer. Eight bits form a standard byte.

Bit Image: A collection of bits in memory that have a rectilinear appearance. The Macintosh screen is a visible bit image.

Bit Map: A pointer to a bit image, the row width of that image, and its boundary rectangle.

Bitwise: Performed bit-by-bit—that is, using bits as they are encountered.

Black Box: A process that produces output from given input which is invisible to the user outside the box.

Boolean: A system of logic that evaluates expressions as true or false. In Pascal, Boolean expressions evaluate to True or False, and all conditional statements evaluate to a Boolean result.

Boot: A process that causes the computer to load, from a disk, an operating system.

Boundary Rectangle: A rectangle that encloses the active area of a bit image and imposes a coordinate system upon it.

Buffer: Something that serves to separate two items. A temporary storage unit that accepts information at one rate and delivers it at another.

Byte: The basic unit of storage. A standard byte contains eight bits and may range in value from 0 to 255.

Call: To begin processing at a designated label or to begin execution through a specific function. The call is most often associated with functions and procedures in Pascal where parameters are used to pass data to the routine.

Character: Any alphanumeric, control character, punctuation, or special symbol that requires one byte of storage space (both in memory and on disk).

Character Height: The vertical height of a character.

Character Image: The bit image that defines a character.

Character Style: A set of stylistic variations such as bold, italic, and underline.

Character Width: The distance the graphics pen moves while drawing one character.

Checked Item: A menu item marked with a check mark.

Click: To position the pointer and briefly press and release the mouse button without moving the mouse.

Close: To remove a window from the screen.

Close Box: A small box to the left of a window's title bar which, when clicked on, closes the window. Also called the go-away region.

Command Key: A special key on the Macintosh keyboard that modifies the character typed. It is frequently used as an alternative to choosing a command in a menu with the mouse.

Compiler: A piece of software designed to translate source programs into object or intermediate code that is taken by a linker to produce executable code.

Constant: A numeric or string quantity that does not change its value throughout program execution.

Content Region: The area of a window that an application draws in.

Control: An object on the screen that causes an action when clicked or dragged. Buttons, dials, and scroll bars are common controls.

Control Character: Any character that causes special processing and occurs between 0 and 31 ASCII.

Control Statement: A statement that directs execution to another portion of the program.

Coordinate Plane: A two-dimensional Cartesian grid with infinitely thin grid lines.

CPU: The acronym for Central Processing Unit. This is the "brain" of the computer and is responsible for all information processing.

Crash: A system malfunction that causes the "bomb" dialog box to appear. The only way to continue using your computer after it crashes is to restart it.

Cursor: A symbol on the screen indicating where the mouse pointer or text insertion point, for example, is located.

Cursor Level: A value that keeps track of the number of times that the cursor has been hidden.

Data: A collection of characters, symbols, or control codes that represent a logical item. The computer differentiates data in memory from program code by its memory location.

Data Base: A large collection of (usually related) information.

Data File: Any named storage location on a disk or similar storage device containing either program code or other data.

Data Structure: A way of organizing collections of data. The data may be of differing data types.

Data Type: One of the classifications for designating data storage and representation.

Datum: A single piece of information. A character, individual field, or individual record, if treated as a unit, can be thought of as a datum.

Deactivate Event: An event that causes a window to become inactive; usually occurs in tandem with an activate event.

Debug: To rid a program of errors. The process one undertakes to ensure program accuracy and completeness.

Declaration Statement: A statement assigning a data type to a variable name.

Default: A value supplied by an application. Usually, default values may be changed by the program's users.

Delete: To remove. Delete applies to files, memory, and text, for example.

Delimiter: To serve as a boundary between two elements. Used to separate fields within a record.

Descent: The vertical distance from a font's baseline to its descent line.

Descent Line: A horizontal line coincident with the bottom of the lowest-reaching characters in a font, including the characters' descenders.

Desktop: The Macintosh metaphor for its operating system called the Finder.

Dialog Box: A type of window opened by an application that needs more information supplied by the user to continue.

Dimension: A property of arrays. A dimension is analogous to a direction in space. One dimension is linear, two dimensions are planar, and three dimensions are cubic.

Dimmed: Drawn in gray rather than in black.

Disabled: A disabled menu item or menu is one that cannot be chosen.

Document Window: A standard Macintosh window for presenting information.

Drag: To press and hold the mouse button while moving the mouse.

Edit: To change or modify information previously entered into an application.

Editor: A word processor, line editor, or other software that can create and alter the contents of a disk file.

Element: One of the members of an array, designated by a unique combination of subscripts.

Empty: Containing no bits as a shape defined by only one point.

Error: A statement or expression that does not follow the syntax regulations for that command. The Pascal interpreter indicates where such syntax errors exist. Logical errors that produce undesired results must be found through execution and debugging.

Event: Notification to an applications program of some event that the program must respond to.

Event Code: An integer representing a particular type of event.

Event Mask: A parameter passed to an Event Manager routine specifying the types of events that the routine is to be applied to.

Event Message: A field of an event record containing event-specific information.

Event Queue: The Event Manager's list of pending events waiting to be processed.

Execute: To run or begin a program.

Exponent: The power of a number. The power of 10 multiplied by the mantissa to yield a notation of the form: n.nnn E exp

Field: A unit containing zero or more characters that are grouped together to form a record. A name, account number, address, or dollar amount can be a field.

File: A logically organized collection of information in which each record, field, or element is related to the other by some criteria.

Font: A complete set of characters of one typeface.

Font Number: The number by which a font is identified.

Font Record: The data structure that contains all of the information needed to describe a font.

Font Size: The size of a font in points.

Frame: To draw a shape by drawing an outline of it.

Function: A Pascal construct that may be activated from a program and returns a value of a specified type.

Global Variable: A variable accessible to all statements within an entire program.

Go Away Region: A synonym for Close box.

GrafPort: A complete drawing environment including such elements as a bit map in which to draw a character font, patterns for drawing and erasing, and other pen characteristics.

Grow Image: The image that appears when resizing a window to indicate the current size of the window.

Handle: A pointer to a master pointer to a dynamic, relocatable data structure.

Hexadecimal: The base 16 numbering system used to represent ASCII characters in one-byte formats. The digits 0 through 9 and the letters A through F are used to represent the numbers 0 through 15.

Highlight: To emphasize something by making it visually distinct from its normal appearance.

Hotspot: The point in a cursor that is aligned with the mouse position.

I/O: The standard abbreviation for input/output.

Icon: A graphics representation of a file, disk, or application.

Inactive Window: Any window that is not the front-most window on the desktop.

Indirection: Referencing by address. Using a variable's address instead of the variable itself. *See also* pointers and handles.

Initialize: In Pascal, to set a variable to a specific value. In the Macintosh Finder, one initializes, or formats, a disk.

Input: The information that comes to the computer from the outside. Input is usually provided to the computer through the mouse or keyboard.

Input/Output: The process of communication between computer, operator, and peripherals.

Insertion Point: Indicates the position at which newly inserted items will be placed.

Integer: A whole numeric value with no fractional component.

Interface: A shared boundary or a piece of hardware used between two pieces of equipment to facilitate communication between them.

Interpreter: An applications program that translates English-like program statements into the native language of the computer.

Invert: To invert the black and white pixels in an image. Inverting is the most common form of highlighting.

Key Code: An integer representing a key on the keyboard or the key pad without reference to the character that key represents.

Key Down Event: An event generated when the user presses a key on the keyboard or key pad.

Key Up Event: An event generated when the user releases a key on the keyboard or key pad.

Keyboard Equivalent: A method of invoking a menu item from the keyboard by holding down the Command key and typing a character.

Keyboard Event: An event generated when a user presses, releases, or holds down a key on the keyboard or key pad.

Kilobyte: 1,024 bytes. From the Greek prefix *kilo,* meaning thousand.

Label: A location within a source program. A program's flow can be altered by directing it to a label within the program itself.

Leading: The amount of blank vertical space between the descent line of one line of text and the ascent line of another line of text.

Linear: Relating to a line, having a single dimension. Contrasted with planar, cubic, etc.

Local Variable: A variable accessible only within a defined block of programming statements.

Logical Expression: An expression yielding True or False.

Logical Operator: An operator used to compare the truth values of two expressions.

Machine Language: A programming language with a very limited instruction set designed to directly control every function of the CPU.

Macintosh Pascal: A Pascal interpreter for creating programs.

MacPaint: An applications program demonstrating the graphics capabilities of the Macintosh.

Macro: An identifier used as synonym for a set of instructions or a constant value.

MacWrite: A word processor for the Macintosh.

Mask: A specific arrangement of bits within a byte used to extract or alter the bits within another byte through the use of Boolean operators.

Matrix: A collection of numbers or characters arranged in rows and columns or higher dimensions. Also known as an array.

Memory: Storage space for data within the computer. Memory is measured in kilobytes (usually in 64K increments).

Menu: A rectangular list of menu items that appears when the user points to and presses a menu title in the menu bar. Dragging through the menu and releasing over a menu item chooses that item.

Menu Bar: The horizontal strip at the top of the Macintosh screen that contains the menu titles of all menus in the menu list.

Menu ID: A positive number that uniquely identifies a menu.

Menu Item: A choice in a menu, usually a command for the current application. In a standard Macintosh menu, a line containing text and possibly an icon.

Menu Item Number: The index starting from 1 of a menu item in a menu.

Menu List: A list of menu handles for all menus in the menu bar. Kept internally by the Menu Manager.

Menu Record: The data structure of a menu where the Menu Manager stores all of the information it needs to perform operations on that menu.

Menu Title: A word or phrase in the menu bar that names a menu.

Metacharacter: A special character used by the Menu Manager to separate menu items or alter their appearance.

Methodology: A means by which an action is performed.

Microprocessor: The microprocessor is responsible for all calculations and hardware controlling functions.

Missing Symbol: A symbol that is drawn in place of a character that is not defined within a particular font.

Mode: The current state of an object discrete from other possible states.

Modifier Key: Special keys on the keyboard that generate no events of their own but change the meanings of other keys. The Shift and Command keys are two examples of modifier keys.

Mouse: A small device used to control the Macintosh. As the mouse is moved around a desk top, it causes corresponding movements of a pointer on the Macintosh screen.

Mouse Button: A rectangular button on top of the mouse. Pressing the mouse button initiates some action at the position of the pointer.

Mouse Button Down Event: An event generated when the user presses the mouse button. (Also called simply "mouse down.")

Mouse Button Up Event: An event generated when the user releases the mouse button. (Also called simply "mouse up.")

Multidimensional: Having more than one dimension.

Nibble: Half of a byte. Four bits.

NIL: A Pascal constant signifying zero.

Null: Used to signify nothing (nothing is not zero).

Null Event: An event returned by the Event Manager when it has no other events to report.

Octal: The base eight numbering system, in which numbers are expressed with the digits 0 through 7.

Operand: A component of an expression that has a value.

Output: The information that goes from the computer to a peripheral. Output is usually displayed on the screen or printer.

Paint: To draw a solid shape.

Parameter: The value or values required by a function or procedure, enclosed within parentheses.

Pascal: A structured programming language developed by Niklaus Wirth.

Pattern: An 8×8 bit image used to define a repeating design or tone.

Pattern Transfer Mode: One of eight transfer modes used for drawing lines or shapes using a pattern.

Pen: A conceptual device used to draw on the Macintosh screen.

Peripheral: Any device connected to a computer that provides input, accepts output, or performs auxiliary functions (such as a storage device).

Picture: A saved sequence of QuickDraw drawing commands that may be replayed through a single procedure call.

Picture Frame: A rectangle that surrounds the picture and provides a frame of reference for scaling the picture.

Pixel: The visual representation of a bit on the screen (white if the bit is 0, black if the bit is 1). The word stems from the contraction of the term picture element.

Plane: The front to back position of a window on the Macintosh screen.

Point: The intersection of a horizontal and vertical grid line on a coordinate plane defined by a horizontal and vertical coordinate.

Pointer: A data type that holds the address of another variable.

Polygon: A sequence of connected lines defined by QuickDraw drawing commands.

Port: Same as a grafPort.

Port Bits: The bit map of a grafPort.

Proportional Font: A font whose characters all have character widths that are proportional to their image widths.

Post: To place an event in the event queue for later processing.

Procedure: A program entity containing statements logically grouped to process one specific task. The procedure may be activated from any section of the program.

Queue: A First-In/First-Out list of items.

RAM: An acronym for Random Access Memory.

Random Access File: A file whose organization and declaration permit access in a random fashion.

Random Access Memory: Memory that is reusable and volatile. Most storage space within the computer is of this type.

Read: To take as input. A program can read from the keyboard, the mouse, a file, or from memory.

Read-Only Memory: Memory that cannot be erased, written on, or changed. Inherent capabilities of the computer and its start-up procedure are stored in Read-Only Memory to provide permanent storage.

Record: A logical grouping of fields in a file. Records are composed of fields. Files are composed of records.

Rectangle: The area defined by two points on a coordinate plane.

Recursion: Something that contains part of itself in its definition.

Recursive Function: A function that may call itself.

Region: An arbitrary area or set of areas on a coordinate plane.

Returned Value: A number or string produced by a function that can be used in an expression or assignment statement.

ROM: An acronym for Read-Only Memory.

Row Width: The number of bytes in each row of a bit image.

Run: To execute a program.

Run Time: Occurring during execution.

Segment: A piece of program, data, etc.

Select: To choose a menu item.

Sequential File: A file whose organization and declaration permit access only in a sequential manner, either from top to bottom, from bottom to top, or from any midpoint to an endpoint.

Size Box: A region usually at the lower right corner of a window that lets the user change the size of the active window.

Solid: Filled in with any pattern.

Source Transfer Mode: One of eight transfer modes for drawing text or transferring any bit image between bit maps.

Structure Region: An entire window. Its complete structure.

Style: See character style.

Subroutine: A procedure to which control can be transferred within a program. Performs one function and returns program flow to the instruction immediately following the call.

Subscript: One of the dimensions of an array. To specify an element of an array, one uses subscripts to identify the unique placement of the element within the array.

Syntax: A statement structure. The arrangement of commands in their proper usage.

System Font: The font, identified by font number 0, that the system uses.

System Font Size: The size of the text drawn by the system using the system font (12 point).

System Window: Any window that is not created by an application. Desk accessories appear in system windows.

Transfer Mode: A specification of which Boolean operation QuickDraw should perform when transferring a bit image from one bit map to another.

Text: Any large body of alphanumeric characters.

Update Event: An event generated by the Window Manager when the update region of a window needs to be redrawn.

Update Region: A window region consisting of all areas of the content region that have to be redrawn.

Variable: Any valid identifier that can change value.

Visible Window: A window that is drawn in its plane on the desktop.

Window: An object on the desktop that presents information.

Window Class: An indication of whether a window is a system window, a dialog or alert window, or a window created by an application.

Window Frame: The structure drawn around the content region of a window by the Window Manager.

Window List: A list of all windows ordered according to their front to back position on the desktop.

Window Manager Port: A grafPort that has the entire screen as its port record and is used by the Window Manager to draw its window frames.

Window Record: A data structure used internally by the Window Manager to store all of the information it needs to perform an operation on a window.

Write: Opposite of read. To write is to send information to a storage device such as memory or file.

I N D E X